SIX PLAYS FOR CHILDREN.

DESIGNED TO INTEREST BOTH ACTORS AND AUDIENCE.

WRITTEN SPECIALLY FOR REPRESENTATION BY CHILDREN,

AND WITH FULL

INSTRUCTIONS FOR IMPROMPTU SCENERY, COSTUMES, AND EFFECTS.

———

By CHAS. HARRISON

(Author of "Amateur Theatricals and Tableaux Vivants").

———

LONDON:
L. UPCOTT GILL, 170, STRAND, W.C.
———
1884.

LONDON: PRINTED BY A. BRADLEY, 170, STRAND, W.C.

TABLE OF CONTENTS.

———

Six Plays for Children.

Introduction.

In writing plays for Theatre Royal Back Drawing Room, the author has two weighty matters to consider. In the first place, he must not rely too much on scenery, or, with few exceptions, on those dramatic mysteries known as "stage effects." The interest of the play is certainly sustained if the smallest scenic representation is produced, which in some cases may be done without much trouble or expense. Thus, if we feel inclined to put the matter in the hands of the costumiers, our drawing room can in a few hours be turned into a fairly commodious theatre, with proscenium, curtain, foot-lights, and enough scenery, on the drop system, to illustrate any ordinary play. But there may be numerous reasons why this step cannot be resorted to, and so the promoters of home plays have to fall back on their artistic and mechanical friends, and to start them making frames and painting scenes. For the latter portion it may be useful to mention that, for home performances, unbleached calico answers very well to paint the scenes on; if this material is fixed on a frame, and primed with a little size and whiting, broken into a pail and boiled, there will be a very fair surface for the amateur scene-painter. The colours used should be what are termed "distemper," and can be obtained of Messrs. Simpson, of London-road, Messrs. Price, of Ebury-street, Pimlico, or Mr. S. French, of 89, Strand. Both Mr. C. H. Fox, of 19, Russell-street, Covent

Garden, and Mr. French, of the Strand, have recently provided for amateurs some scenery on strong paper, in the form of sheets, which can be fastened together, or pasted on cardboard or wood. The idea is a particularly happy one, with only one disadvantage, and that is the cost price; thus, his terms for the number of sheets to make up a cottage interior are 40s. to 50s., while a garden, a wood, and a drawing-

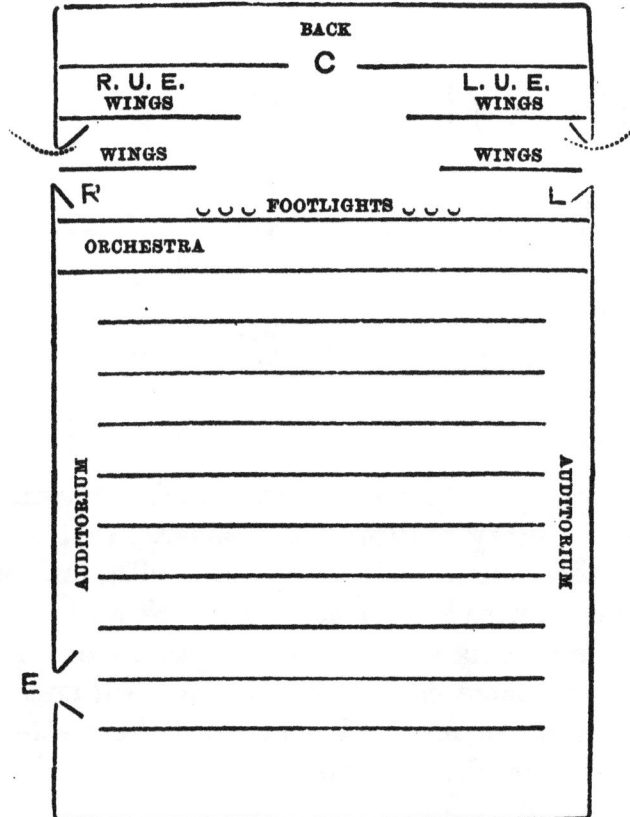

STAGE DIRECTIONS:

R—Right.   L Left.   C—Centre.   R U E—Right Upper Entrance.   L U E—Left Upper Entrance.   E—Entrance to Auditorium.

PLAN OF ROOM, ARRANGED FOR THEATRICALS.

room scene each range about the same price. Much cheaper are the sundry articles on the same system, namely, a door for drawing room or cottage, a practical window and fireplace, for 5s. Paper is also supplied for a proscenium, which can be pasted on three boards, at 1s. per sheet; this, however, is not actually necessary, as curtains hung at the folding doors will answer all purposes.

The arrangement of the stage must be left mainly to circumstances, but the plan shown on p. 2 might be applied to any ordinary room. It is, however, wise not to be too exacting as to the points for the entrances and exits. With this view, I have avoided, as much as possible, any positive directions as to where the characters come on and go off. I should always advise a pair of practical curtains at the front of the stage; these, if fixed with rings on a brass or iron rod, can be quickly drawn by means of a string.

The proper rehearsing of the play, however fragile or flimsy in plot or dialogue, is one of the steps for ensuring success; if the children are drilled into their parts with regularity they will warm more to their work than if the piece were rehearsed by spasmodic efforts, and after long and uncertain intervals. The stage manager, no matter whether it is papa, uncle, or cousin, must possess tact and judgment, and enforce, to a certain extent, discipline with his little players. He should see that entrances and exits are made at the proper cue, that no additions are made to the dialogue without his sanction; he must arrange his scenery, if any, and his properties, so as to avoid that dramatic bugbear, a "wait;" and this call for tact and judgment is necessary in distributing the parts among his players with due regard to the abilities and style required for giving a generally good representation of the characters. While the play is being rehearsed, all the actors should be followed by a book, and any suggestion as to business or acting should be marked there and then on the actor's part.

Music is of great advantage in a home play, where scenes are more to be imagined than practically represented. With this view, it would be well for the manager to secure the services of a musical friend who would take an interest in the rehearsals, and go through the songs, &c., at the same time following out those portions where music would be acceptable. To assist musician and actors, I have given, in the following plays, a few bars of the airs mentioned, and also the names of the publishers from whom the complete pianoforte scores can be obtained. For chords—music to bring on or take off a character—the cues should be marked and given to the pianist to act upon. It is necessary to fix the cue on a child's attention, and this may be more quickly brought about by writing out the parts in the following style, say:

—————————————————————————follow not!

So AND So. Yet, for all this, I'll watch the path he takes,
And still attempt to save him.

If a line is made leading up to the cue, and a deep one under-neath, this will greatly help the little actor to retain that which, if forgotten or spoken out of place, will cause a block, and set the acting all out of gear.

It may not be out of place to mention that all wigs, masks, and make-ups can be obtained on hire from Clarkson, Welling-ton-street, Strand; Nash, of Chandos-street; and Fox, of Russell-street. These firms will send a man experienced in the art of "making up," should it be deemed advisable to go in for realism; and any gold or silver ornaments, fringe or lace, can be procured of White, 21, Bow-street, Covent Garden; while portable theatres can be hired of Simmons, Coventry-street, Fox, of Russell-street, Covent Garden, and Avery, of Great Portland-street. With regard to costumes, directions are given, preceding the plays, for dressing each character; and though costumes may be hired from any theatrical costumier, I have endeavoured to show that it is possible, with a handy needlewoman and a few yards of cheap stuff, to make up something which, if not strictly correct, will cause amusement, and add to the completeness of the entertainment. Magnesium light will be found remarkably effective, and can be obtained in numerous colours of S. French, 89, Strand, price 1s. each.

LITTLE CINDERELLA.

CHARACTERS.

CAROLINE.
BELLA. } *Sisters to* CINDERELLA.
CINDERELLA.

THE FAIRY.
THE PRINCE.

GUESTS, COURTIERS, MAIDENS, &c.

COSTUMES.

CINDERELLA.—Modern dress, with red or pink handkerchief over shoulders, short frock with red stockings, rather dilapidated appearance, tattered and patched.

CAROLINE AND BELLA.—As gaudy and gorgeous as possible; a few yards of pompadour cretonne would make an excellent showy skirt; shoes with large rosettes, and any finery, such as feathers and old laces, should be added. In making the skirt, a little caricature on the current eccentricity of fashion would provoke amusement. A profusion of jewellery and huge cretonne fans would be decidedly appropriate, while something pronounced in the way of head dresses should not be omitted.

THE FAIRY.—A simple costume of muslin, with any trimmings of light blue or pink ribbons, a gold sash and head dress, with long wand (*i.e.,* a thin rod covered with gold paper). A number of gold and silver stars, such as sold for ornamenting Christmas trees, would answer admirably for decorating the dress.

THE PRINCE.—A silk or satin hat trimmed with feathers, lace ruffles, tunic, costume of cretonne; or a coloured cloak thrown over an ordinary knickerbocker suit, with deep frills of lace round legs and sleeves.

GUESTS, COURTIERS, &c.—Remnants of the wardrobe should be

called into requisition in decking out these. Old robes, dressing gowns, opera cloaks, &c., should be brought in, to give animation and a bit of colouring to the scene.

———

SCENE I.—A KITCHEN.

With large fireplace, plain deal table, dishes on shelves, and dish covers hanging against the wall; the ordinary drawing-room grate will answer if a frame is quickly put together of match lining, and painted a dull stone colour. The drawing room furniture should, to some extent, be removed, and a certain amount of kitchen things scattered about the room. If it is necessary to keep the carpet down, strips of oilcloth should be laid along the floor. A dresser could be easily made up by having a long board fixed on two trestles; the inside of the bottom should be hung with black lining, and pots and kettles placed on. Over the long board should be laid a white cloth, and the usual tureens and crockery arranged on it. For the shelves, with plates, &c., it is always best to make a frame, size of the board representing the bench of the dresser; this could be covered with unbleached calico, and primed with size and whiting mixed in a pail. The surface for painting being ready, the shelves and plates can be easily drawn and painted in, the pattern on the china merely requiring to be indicated rather than painted in; this frame could be hung against the wall, the board on trestles meeting it, while the join can, of course, be hidden by the tureens and crockery previously mentioned. A fire is in the grate, with large kettle on, and as the scene opens CINDERELLA *is discovered sweeping up the hearth.*

> CIND. Scrub, wash, and clean, from morn till night!
> I feel, this evening, worn out quite.
> Though I've two sisters, one can see
> They pile all drudgery on me.
> They order and compel me to
> Be quick about the work I do;
> If not—then harsh and unkind snapping,
> And, worse than all, then comes a slapping.
> In truth, I am a maiden all forlorn,
> With dirty face and clothes all torn,
> While my two sisters, with papa's cash,
> In gorgeous dresses cut a dash.
> Their costumes cost too much, I'm sure!

[Bell rings violently.

> A ring! (*looks out of window*)—a prince's carriage at the
> door!
> This shows our family is rising in position,
> While I am kept in such a low condition!

[Great confusion and bustling outside.

Enter CAROLINE *and* BELLA.

CAR. Now, Cinderella, quick! hear what I've to say,
　And don't stand staring in that lazy way!
　What do you think? I'm sure you'll be delighted—
BELLA. To the King's ball we've been invited!
　A certain evidence we're much admired;
　But, to the point, young person; you're required
　To dress us both, and do your duty
　In showing up our points of beauty.
CAR. And quickly, Miss! or, to your sorrow,
　You'll have no butter for your tea to-morrow;
　For, who knows, but that the Prince might see
　A blushing, beautiful Princess in me!
BELLA. Or else in me! I've heard it said
　I'm only fit to wear a crown upon my head;
　But, come! our time is short; why let us wait,
　When, Caroline, the ball begins at eight?

CAROLINE, BELLA, *and* CINDERELLA. *Position each side of*
　CINDERELLA, *whom they occasionally rap.*

CAR. Now, make haste! Cinderella,
　　And brush my satin dress!
BELLA. And don't forget my blue brocade—
　　It's in an awful mess.
CAR. And put new lace upon the cuffs;
BELLA. And also iron out the ruffs.
CAR. Remember, too, the cloaks and muffs,
BOTH. 　　You slowcoach, Cinderella!
CIND. I'll put new lace upon the cuffs,
　　And also iron out the ruffs;
　　I'll not forget the cloaks and muffs
　　　For Caroline and Bella.
CAR. Now, hurry, Cinderella,
　　To Jones's in the Square,
BELLA. And ask him if he'll send us
　　Some pomatum for our hair.
CAR. And go to Jenkin's, in the lane,
　　And borrow a bouquet again.
　　Now, run your hardest might and main,
　　　You slowcoach Cinderella!
BOTH. 　　You slowcoach, Cinderella!

　　　[*The sisters push* CINDERELLA, *and exeunt* OMNES.
　　　*The stage is darkened slightly, and slow music
　　　brings* CINDERELLA *on again, looking very
　　　dejected.*

CIND. I've dressed them out in silks and laces,
　　And powdered, too, their hair, and faces—
　　Made bows, rosettes, and tiddivated
　　All articles dilapidated.
　　They looked so grand, papa declared
　　The tradesmen looked, the neighbours stared!

But now, they're to the palace gone,
I feel so sad, and so forlorn!
(*Weeping.*)   They are so cruel—it breaks my heart
To think I play a servant's part—
With ne'er a kindly word nor look—
With ne'er a toy or picture book
This round of dreary life to cheer—
I feel, I feel (*cries*)—Oh, dear! Oh, dear!

Enter FAIRY.

[*If a little blue magnesium light is burnt
here the effect will be very pretty.*

FAIRY. Come dry your tears, my little maid!
Don't start; I hope you're not afraid!
It's true I came in unexpected,
But you'll no longer look dejected—
When you hear what I'm going to do,
To make you glad and happy too.
CIND. (*astonished*). Did you come through the coal-hole or the area?
(*Aside.*)   What lovely clothes! she's like a fairy!
FAIRY. Your sisters are unkind, I know your trouble well.
CIND. That's very strange! for who could tell?
FAIRY. They slap you, snub your manners and your clothes;
CIND. They also snub my looks, and snub my nose!
FAIRY. No longer they shall treat you in a manner so unkind.
Hey, Presto!   Fetch the largest pumpkin you can find—

[CINDERELLA *fetches pumpkin and places it on floor.*

And place it on the table here.   Now look outside the door
And tell me what you see.
CIND.   A splendid coach! Oh, lor!
It's beautiful!   Why, I declare,
Fit for a prince, or a lord mayor!
How beautifully it's made!   Are you the maker?
FAIRY. Yes; and a party in Long Acre.
Now fetch the mousetrap.   These six mice inside

[CINDERELLA *hands mousetrap.*

I change to horses, prancing side by side!
And now that rattrap, and its victim too,

[*Waves her wand over rattrap.*

I change to a coachman, with his cocked hat too!
CIND. Is this a dream! this wondrous transformation?

[*Looks out of window.*

And yet it seems to cause a wonderful sensation.
FAIRY. Now for the footmen, we must see about them;
As the tradesmen say, no carriage is complete without them.
And now six lizards from the garden fetch.
CIND. Six lizards! well, they're rather hard to catch.

[*Exit, and enter with lizards.*

In the garden I caught them just to hand.

FAIRY. I change these now to footmen grand,

CIND. And who's this carriage for? a noble, I suppose?

FAIRY. In truth, to take you to the ball!

CIND.   What! in these clothes?

FAIRY. No! Away with this old tattered gown, away!—
A relic from the rag bag, I should say.

CIND. (*slips off old gown*). Oh! what a beauty! I've never seen
A satin with such a glossy sheen.
What would my sisters say? Perhaps
They'd show their admiration in some slaps?
                         [*Looks in glass.*

I do look nice, and on my face
Of dirt or smut there's not the slightest trace,
And that's so strange for me. I'm sure
It's not been washed for a week or more.
Oh, thank you, lady!

FAIRY.   No thanks; but let me tell
How you're to spend this evening happily and well.
For that carriage and the horses now waiting at the gate
Will bear you to the ball. You'll only be a trifle late.
But mark on what condition this transformation's made!

CIND. (*aside*). Condition! There's something awful coming, I'm afraid.

FAIRY. I'm your fairy godmother, and your protector too,
So that will just explain the interest I take in you.

CIND. Yes, truly so; for did any little lass
E'er find herself so nicely dressed, with slippers, too, of glass!

Song, FAIRY—*air*, "*He was a careful Man*" (J. Bath).

CHORUS.

Now start, dear Cinderella!
    But mind that you are here
Upon the very stroke of twelve,
    Or else you'll find, my dear,
No carriage with its cushions,
    And its trimmings, and its lace,
But that very self-same pumpkin
    Reclining in its place!

Chorus.

Now, be a careful girl;
Now, be a careful girl!
    Mind you are here.

CIND.   Oh! never fear,
    I'll be a careful girl!

FAIRY. The horses which are prancing,
    And look so very nice,
Would instantly resume their forms
    Of timid little mice;
While that obliging coachman,
    With his livery so pat,
Would suddenly go back into
    The semblance of a rat!

                                [*Chorus.*

Your footmen, quite perfection,
    As a lord mayor would agree,
Would change to scaly lizards,
    Quite detestable to see!   [*Patting* CINDERELLA
And this handsome little lady,   *under chin.*
    In her flowers and her lace,
Would be ragged Cinderella,
    With her dirty little face!   [*Chorus.*

    [*Exeunt* FAIRY *and* CINDERELLA *to lively music,*
        after which a lot of cheering is heard at side.

SCENE II.—BALL ROOM.

Red magnesium light, Japanese lanterns hung about. Curtains made of cheap cretonne, draped at different portions of the room. In one of the corners a throne should be arranged for the King and Queen (i.e., two chairs placed on a packing case and covered with some showy material. Some of the guests should be standing in groups, but as the scene opens a quadrille or minuet should be danced. The properties used in the previous scene must be cleared away rapidly, to avoid anything like a tedious "wait"—wearisome enough to grown-up people, but positively terrible to a juvenile audience. The clearance of the properties is a great feature, and should be rehearsed nearly as much as the acting.

*BELLA and CAROLINE come down stage, and are casting spiteful
glances at CINDERELLA, who is chatting with the PRINCE.*

BELLA. A very forward person, I am sure!
    I should think her company an awful bore.
CAR. The way she flirts, and smiles, and giggles,
    And goes through most fantastic wriggles,
    Does not betoken much high breeding.
BELLA. You're right! She's evidently needing
    A chaperone of strong determination,
    To teach *our* art of fascination!
CAR. The Prince seems quite attracted, Bella, dear.
BELLA. I wonder, too, when there's such beauty here!
CAR. She's very plain.
BELLA.   And most precocious!
CAR. Her style is certainly atrocious.
BELLA. Her dress is common to the very tape.
CAR. I never saw a nose so bad a shape;
    And eyes like ferrets, I declare!
    And mark the ginger tint of hair!
BELLA. I've not danced with the Prince this evening yet,
    He seems quite taken with his pet.
CAR. A common person—some one from the town!
    Her name, no doubt, is Smith or Brown.   [*They stroll up.*

            [*The PRINCE and CINDERELLA stroll down.*

PRINCE. Of poetry I've only just a smattering,
    But really you are——
CIND.   Oh! you're too flattering;
    And, Prince, excuse me if I tell you pat,
    I look upon a flatterer as a flat.
PRINCE. And yet I speak the truth, I do suppose,
    When I compare you to the rose;
    In fact, I think your manners charming!
CIND. Your sentiments are quite alarming.
    But, come! we are observed; and I declare
    Some ladies want you over there!
PRINCE. I fain would linger with one so nice!
CIND. I should, your Highness, like an ice,
    A nice Bath bun, some pastry stuff,
    A sponge cake, and three-cornered puff.
PRINCE. I fly to order your repast!   [*Exit.*
CIND. I'm very glad he's gone at last,
    For though so nice in manner and in bearing,
    It's meet that I should be preparing
    For my journey. (*Looks at watch.*) Oh, horror!
    It wants but sixty seconds to to-morrow!
    I'll start at once, without even one adieu,
    And leave my opera cloak and pastry too!

        [*Rushes excitedly through crowd of guests, and leaves one
            shoe on stage. The guests here go through a short
            dance to lively music, after which enter the PRINCE
            with a tray full of pastry, ices, &c.*

PRINCE. She's vanished! I've searched the palace o'er,
From the cellar to the attic door!
The battlements, the cloisters, and the lobbies,
Assisted by my father's palace bobbies.
In all the chambers and the kitchen,
Yet not a particle of that bewitching
Creature could I get a glimpse!
I feel fatigued.   (*To waiter*.)   Some tea and shrimps!

Song, PRINCE—*air*, "*Mistletoe Bough*."

CHORUS. *ad lib.*

a tempo.

I'm utterly staggered, dumbfounded as well,
At the sudden departure of this pretty belle;
I've asked all the guests and the courtiers as well,
But nowhere is she to be seen!

Chorus, OMNES.

Oh! Where has she gone to?
Oh! Where has she gone?

I've searched everywhere, but I can't anyhow
Discover the ghost of her shadow just now;
Perhaps, like the girl in the Mistletoe Bough,
She's shut herself up in a chest!   [*Chorus.*

[GUESTS *repeat Chorus and dance a breakdown. At
the end of Chorus the* PRINCE *suddenly discovers*
CINDERELLA'S *slipper.*

PRINCE. Good gracious! here's a pretty pass!
A lady's slipper, made of glass!
The owner must be in a pretty plight,
Now one slipper's left—the other right!
Oh, what a charming foot! it's what I call
Perfection, it's so shapely and so small;
Now guests! I beg you cease your conversation,
Just while I make this proclamation!

[*All the* GUESTS *come round the* PRINCE,
the KING *and* QUEEN *on either side.*

PRINCE. Whereas some lady hath lost her shoe while dancing in this
　　　　 ball room, and this is to give notice, that it is the intention
　　　　 of his Royal and Most Imperial Highness, to take as
　　　　 Princess the lady who can produce the fellow, and wear
　　　　 the said shoe, without undue pressure!

GUESTS. Hurrah! hurrah!

　　　　　　　[CAROLINE and BELLA struggle past the other LADIES.

BELLA. Your Highness, it will fit me to a T,
　　　　 I'm certain of it!

CAR. 　　　　　　　Say, rather me!

PRINCE. I won't dispute your claims, but trust you'll wait
　　　　 Until to-morrow, when, at eight,
　　　　 The competition will begin it.

BELLA. I'm confident that I shall win it!

PRINCE. Now, guests, resume the dancing—be elastic,
　　　　 Nimble, and lively on the "light fantastic."

　　　　　　　[The GUESTS go through a dance as the Curtain falls.

————

SCENE III.—KITCHEN, AS BEFORE.

CINDERELLA discovered.　　Slow music as curtain rises.

Sings.

Ever scrubbing,
Ever rubbing,
Rubbing dirty saucepans bright!
Water boiling,
Ever toiling,
From the morn until the night!
Papa calling,
Sisters bawling,
Tradesmen ringing at the back;
Always at it,
Drat it! drat it!
Always tired, always black!

Enter CAROLINE and BELLA.

BELLA (*to* CAR.). Audacious! she's singing songs!
　　　　 Pray, have you cleaned my curling tongs?

CIND. I haven't; I have been so sickly.

BELLA. Come, hurry, Miss, and clean them quickly!
　　　　 You're getting lazier, I declare!

CIND. Won't paper do to curl your hair?

　　　　　　　[BELLA and CAROLINE horrified at this suggestion.

BELLA. I really feel inclined to smack her.
　　　　 Curl papers, indeed! (*slaps* CINDERELLA)—come, there's a
　　　　　　　cracker!

CAR. Come, let us go, my Bella dear!
　　　　 It is not meet for us to stop down here.

What would the Prince say, did he but know
His favourites patronised the kitchen so!

BELLA. Ah! true, sweet Kate! but did you see
How constantly he smiled on me?

CAR. He blushed whene'er he met my eye,
And kissed my hand.

BELLA.   He did! Oh, fie!
Ah, Cinderella! you little know
How we are petted when we go
To parties, balls, five o'clock teas!
We're looked upon as quite the cheese.

[*A loud and important knock is heard at the door.*

CAR. Good gracious! whoe'er can it be?
We're awfully dirty, a visitor to see!

[CINDERELLA *opens door, and enter* PRINCE, KING,
QUEEN, *and* SUITE; *one of the attendants bears the
slipper on a cushion.*

PRINCE. Good morning, ladies! I've dropped in to see
If I can find the owner of this property;

[*Shows slipper, and* CINDERELLA *starts.*

Or, better still, the lady who with ease
Can wear this slipper without a squeeze;
As yet no lady has been found
With foot so small, tho' I'll be bound
A few have tried to, with a pinch or two,
Reduce their feet by quite an inch or two.
Now, ladies, try! and if 'twill fit,
Remember the reward of it!

[CAROLINE *first struggles to get it on, but fails.*

BELLA. Allow me, your Highness, and all will see
How easily it goes on me.

[*Struggles to get the shoe on, but fails.*

Oh, what a nuisance!

CAR.   An awful shame!

BELLA. Our reputation's gone!

CAR.   So has our name!

PRINCE. Come then, my lords! we'll try next door—

[*Looking at* CINDERELLA.

But, stay, I've passed this lady o'er—
Pray, who are you?

CIND.   I'm Cinderella, Sir!

PRINCE. What, ho! the slipper. (*Aside.*) It seems suited more
to her.

CAR. (*to* CINDERELLA). I'll make you smart for this!

BELLA.   ·   And so will I!

CAR. How dare you catch the Prince's eye!
You're only a drudge, Miss, of the kitchen!

BELLA. She's awful!

PRINCE. (*aside*).   Say, rather, bewitching!

[*The slipper is tried on, and fits beautifully.*

PRINCE. With this little fit so ends our play;
There's nothing more I have to say,
Excepting to express my thanks,
In following out our little pranks,
While endeavouring to portray
The very cruel and unkind way
Poor Cinderella has been treated.

CIND. I've triumphed in the long run, you'll agree—
The true reward of plain humility.
It's true I had to scour, clean, and scrub,
And, goodness knows, I've often had a snub!
But that's forgotten now, and I am sure
We won't revert to that behaviour any more.
Now, sisters, let me kiss you both, and say,
I trust that it will wash all jealousies away!

[*Kisses* CAROLINE *and* BELLA.

When I'm princess you'll come and see
Us every Sunday?—come to tea—
Oh, dinner—breakfast—supper too!—
And bring papa to have a cup or two.

[*Enter* FAIRY.

Why, here's my fairy godmother! I guess,
Come to see the climax of our happiness.
Oh, let me shower you with thanks! you kind—

[CINDERELLA *takes her by the hand.*

FAIRY. A shower! I've left my umbrella behind—
Well, well, no thanks to me, my dear, are needed,
I'm only glad to find that you've succeeded!

Finale—air, "*Oh! dem Golden Slippers!*" (Pitman, Paternoster Row).

PRINCE. Oh, we're going far away, to a palace miles away!
And we'll leave the dingy kitchen for ever and a day!

CAR. *and* BELLA. While we're sorry in our heart for the very naughty part
We have taken in scolding Cinderella every day!

CIND. But I'm sure you all will say, it's a very happy way
To clear a family squabble up, for squabbles do not pay.

FAIRY. While the moral will be seen, not to be stuck up and mean,
Which, I hope, my friends in front will quite agree.

Chorus, OMNES.

Oh, those crystal slippers !
Oh, those crystal slippers !
Crystal slippers sweet Cinderella wore upon her feet !
Oh, those crystal slippers !
Oh, those crystal slippers !
Pattering, pattering, glittering, glittering, down the busy street !

Repeat Chorus, and Curtain.

Beauty and the Beast.

———

CHARACTERS.

De Nogo ....A Speculative Merchant.
Softpate ....His Clerk.
Sir Beastus Bearing...........The——
Beauty ....⎫
Plaineye ....⎬ De Nogo's Daughters,
Passbye ....⎭

ATTENDANTS, &C.

———

COSTUMES.

De Nogo.—Dress in Scene I.: A nap hat, huge red comforter, long robe or cloak, two umbrellas in hands, railway rug, and a large carpet bag. Scene II.: Very ragged; carries an empty carpet bag, an old bundle, and an umbrella absurdly broken; should wear an old hat, minus crown or brim; a hungry appearance is necessary, and this can be represented by slightly shading the hollows of the eyes and cheekbones with a little powdered burnt cork. Scene III.: He is supposed to have come back to prosperity, and should look ridiculously gorgeous, with an enormous coloured bow at his neck, a coat made of pompadour cretonne, or similar stuff, broad sash, and a big golden eyeglass (*i.e.*, cut out of cardboard).

Softpate.—Scene II.: In the same plight as his master; should have a very large bag, and a very ragged handkerchief, which they share between them when they weep; an old cloak or coat, tattered and patched with large pieces of blue and red stuff. Scene III.: He is nearly as gorgeous as his master.

Sir Beastus Bearing.—A head-dress of an old wool mat, or better still, a November mask in the form of a beast. (Capital masks can be obtained of Clarkson, Wellington-street, Strand, W.C.; or Nash, Chandos-street.) An old circular fur cloak would make a very good coat ; while the second dress, when transformed to a Prince, could be made of red stuff, tunic shape, sash, and knee breeches.

BEAUTY.—A silk or muslin dress, trimmed with a little gold or silver lace, jaunty cap of silk or satin, with large feather, long silk mittens, bracelets, and fan.

PLAINEYE AND PASSBYE.—Similar to above, only slightly plainer in appearance.

SCENERY.

SCENE I.—ORDINARY DRAWING ROOM.

SCENE II.—EXTERIOR OF BEASTUS' PALACE.

This could be made fairly effective by having the form of red brick walls painted on sheets of cardboard, and then fixed on a frame, with a green bank coming from the bottom. Near to the side of the stage could be indicated a portion of the gate, with large bell handle ; or the scene could be painted with distemper colours on unbleached calico stretched on a frame and primed with size and whiting ; all the plants in the house should be used to back up the wall. If in flower-pots, a strip of board painted green or earth colour should be placed in front.

SCENE III.—INTERIOR OF BEASTUS' PALACE.

Curtains of cretonne over throne (i.e., arm chair covered with red twill), rugs on floor, plants in jars on each side.

SCENE I.—ORDINARY DRAWING ROOM.

DE NOGO, *ready for his journey, and his three* DAUGHTERS *discovered.*

DE NOGO. Come ! dry your eyes, my daughters true—
　　　　Such tearful habits you will rue—
　　　　Bad for the constitution, I've always heard.
DAUGHTERS. It's very foolish !
DE NOGO. 　　　　　　　　It's absurd !
　　　　I go to make my fortune ; one would think,
　　　　By all your tears, I stood upon the brink
　　　　Of some misfortune.　So dry your eyes,
　　　　And pack my sandwiches and pies,

Some Cadbury's Cocoa, Reckitt's Blue,
Some almond rock, and hair oil too!

[Two Sisters PASSBYE *and* PLAINEYE *exeunt.*

While as to you, my Beauty, sweet,
I'll bring you something nice to eat—
A foreign bun, or Continental acid drop,
A skipping-rope, or else a humming-top.
But if my specs they turn out lucky,
I'll bring rare jewels, my little ducky—
Big diamonds, rubies, sapphires, pearls,
For you, most beautiful of girls!
That will please you, I suppose.

BEAUTY. Thanks, papa! I'd sooner have a rose.
Through floral glades I like to range—
I'm, oh! so fond of flowers!

DE NOGO.   That's not strange;
But still, Miss, in the present age,
Jewels, not flowers, are the rage.
A girl refuse a trinket! quite surprising—
Some girls for jewels are tantalising.
You know your taste, Miss, I suppose.

BEAUTY. I'd just as lief, papa, have a rose.

DE NOGO. I'll not forget your wishes, Beauty, dear,
Also your sisters—why, they're here!

Enter PASSBYE *and* PLAINEYE.

PASS. Here's your parcels, tightly packed,
So that the jars will not get cracked.

DE NOGO. Thanks, dearest children; but, ah! my comb!
'Twill remind me of the *parting* here at home,
And, though no sons, I've three daughters fair;
So get the comb, 'twill serve me for the *hair.*

*[*PASSBYE *gets comb in a case.*

Now for a change of air, of scene, of home,
O'er mountains, deserts, furrin' parts to roam!
I'll roam.

BEAUTY *(weeping).*   Will you be long away?

DE NOGO. Well, "Rome was not built in a day;"
And things I have to do will take
A goodish time; so, daughters, make
Yourselves at home! Don't run the water-rate;
But, as to rent, well, let 'em wait!
Pay all the bills, and when you're axed to,
Clear up my awful Income Tax too!
Bolt all the doors at night, put up the chains too,
Do what you can. And now my train's due.
When I return with presents I will load you,
And pay up all back debts I've owed you.
Oh! if my specs are but successful, then
I shall come back one of the richest men!

Quartette, DE NOGO, BEAUTY, PLAINEYE, *and* PASSBYE — *air*, "*We are a Merry Family*" (Francis Bros. and Day).

DE NOGO. Now, let me go, my daughters three;
        I won't be long away.
BEAUTY. Oh! papa, I shall weep for thee,
        In spite of what you say.
PLAIN. Oh! bring us back some nicies, pa!
        A diamond ring or two.
PASS. A model boat or tramway car!
DE NOGO.   I'll see what I can do.

            [DE NOGO *embraces all his* DAUGHTERS
                     as the Curtain falls.

SCENE II.—EXTERIOR OF BEASTUS' PALACE.

A chord of tragic music should be played on the piano, with a distant rumbling, supposed to emanate from the BEAST, *as the Curtain rises,* DE NOGO *enters very dejected, leaning on his umbrella, and looking about with a hungry gaze.*

DE NOGO. Where am I? what am I? Well may I ask.
        To give an answer would be a sorry task.
        This is the thirty-thousandth mile
        I've tramped o'er in this sorry style!
        A kind of ragged scarecrow rover!   [*Pointing to clothes.*
        This is a style I can't get over.

All enterprises failures; every spec, too;
And only what you might expect, too!
For Fortune has deserted me; Fortune, fickle,
Has brought me to this pretty pickle.
The mention of that word, ah! makes me pine
For something in the eating line.
I'm sadly off for wittles here;
There's no sign of a café near,
And if there was, it's very clear
I couldn't dine—at least to-day,
Because—well, I couldn't pay.

[Looks round.   A groan heard outside.

But what is this—some grand estate?
Ah, ah! my clerk and counsellor, Softpate!

Enter SOFTPATE, *very fatigued.*

SOFT. Oh, dear! oh, lor! I'm famished quite;
I've struggled on with all my might
Until I'm done up.   Alack the day
That from my home I came away!   *[Weeps.*
DE NOGO. All may go well, so why despond?
Of looking on the black side you're too fond.
Why not be gay? for who may tell,
We may win yet!
SOFT.   That's very well;
But, still, I'm much inclined to think
It may be ill with nought to eat nor drink.
DE NOGO. I'm rather faint myself.
SOFT.   Faint's not the word!
Say, rather, starving!
DE NOGO.   Bah! absurd!
You had some tea last Tuesday night,
Some dinner on the day before!
SOFT.   Yes, quite right!
But that's five days ago, and one feels
Such intervals between your meals
Are rather irksome.
DE NOGO.   Alas! too true!
BOTH. Whatever are we going to do?
DE NOGO. What will my daughters think?
SOFT.   My mother, too!
DE NOGO. Rare jewels I promised them, and one a rose,
Sweetstuff, fancy stuff, and foreign clothes,
All kinds of nick-nacks, such as you meet
In every kind of Continental street.
But nick-nacks cost money, and, to put it pat,
I've yet to learn the *knack* of making that.

[They both sit down in centre of stage.

DE NOGO. What had we better do?
SOFT.   How can I say?

DE NOGO. This travelling's a myth.

SOFT.   It doesn't pay!

DE NOGO (*suddenly starting up and dancing round the stage*). Ha, ha!
    —a bright idea—
    A brilliant one, as you shall hear!
    We both have voices, full of charms;
    Our legs are tired.   Let's sing for alms,
    Or, plainer speaking, sing for pence!

SOFT. Anything better than this suspense!

> [*They put their hats on the ground, and while they are
> singing a few people get round, but all leave the stage
> just before the finish of the song.*

Duett, DE NOGO *and* SOFTPATE—*air, " Dear Little Innocent Things."*

CHORUS.

    We're all the way from London town,
        It's easy for to see;
    At present we are rather down,
        And deep in poverty.

DE NOGO. I came to make my fortune here,
        Go home a millionaire;

SOFT. But somehow money don't appear,
        And so we are *a pair*.

Chorus.

Of poor struggling, travelling folks, Oh, dear!
    We crave a small copper from anyone here;
A crust we could munch, or those biscuits called Lunch,
    Oh, pity our helpless condition, Oh, dear!

So kindly, strangers, spare a penny
    To help us on our way,
Because, alas! we have not any
    Our landlady to pay.
Don't turn a deaf ear to our prayer,
    But drop your coppers in;
This is no usual beggar's snare,
    But truly genuine!

(*Spoken*) And help a pair——   [*Chorus.*

De Nogo. Just like the usual crowd, they fly
    When the solicitous hat comes by.
    Not a copper! How are you?   [*Looks in hat.*
    Soft.   Not e'en a sou!

                                                       [*Finds something.*

    But hold! there's something at the bottom shining.
De Nogo. Have you got it?
    Soft.   No; it's in the lining.

        [*They go through some comic business
               in trying to tear the hat inside out.*

    Now for it! I've got it to the top!
    It must be a sovereign.
    Both (*disappointed*).   No, an acid drop!
De Nogo. No matter, we no longer famished feel.
    Let's enjoy a sweetstuff meal!

        [*They divide the acid drop and begin to look round.*

    (*Looking towards flowers.*) A bed of roses! Now then to pluck
    A stunner for my little duck!
    So pleased——

        [*Plucks a rose; a terrible growl and crash is heard, and
           Sir Beastus just pops his head in at side; they drop
           their luggage and clutch each other in abject terror.*

De Nogo (*trembling*). I hear a shout!
    Is there a railway anywhere about?   [*Looks up.*
    Perhaps there's a collision, or a smash,
    Or a gas explosion!—I heard a crash.
    Someone broke their bootlace!
    Soft.   Or dropped their stud,
    Their watch, or watch-chain in the mud!
De Nogo. A window smashed, perhaps! or else a youthful scamp
    Has smashed the skylight.
    Soft.   Or the lamp!

                                    [*Another growl heard.*

    Oh, dear! I shoudn't wonder
    If we don't have a storm.
De Nogo.   And that's the thunder!
    Soft. In that case we ought to find a doorway or a portico.
    What do you say?
De Nogo.   Oh, yes; we "ought to go!"

[*They gather up their luggage, and are walking out arm-in-arm, when* SIR BEASTUS *confronts them; they start back and fall on their knees.*

DE NOGO *and* SOFT. Alas! some awful animal or ogie!
   Or else the local village bogie!
   Oh, kind Sir, we are poor strangers two!
BEASTUS. T—t—tremble!
 BOTH (*shivering*).   We do, we do!
BEASTUS. Prepare for every kind of torture,
   Since on my grand estab' I've caught yer.
   You'd steal my roses—have you not seen
   My notice-board upon the green,
   Which mentions penalties for such an act?
   In short, to a dungeon you'll be packed,
   And when I'm hungry, both of you,
   I'll have made up into a stew;
   Or else you will be boiled or roasted,
   Though Englishmen are often toasted!
SOFT. *and* DE NOGO. Oh, kind and noble Sir, pray pause!
DE NOGO. And hear why I transgressed your laws!
BEASTUS. Enough! there is the certain fact;
   I caught you in the very act!
   Such wanton acts I've always hated.
DE NOGO. But hear how we were actuated!
BEASTUS. Tut, tut! poor tramp, do you suppose
   I cultivated that 'ere rose
   For you to take, to steal, to pluck?
   It's just my hobby——
 BOTH.   And it's just our luck!
   Think, after years we have been toiling,
   To be in such a stew!——
BEASTUS.   Prepare for boiling!
   I'm getting hungry—in fact, I feel
   Quite ready for my morning meal.
DE NOGO (*weeping*). What will they do at home without their pa?
   I have three daughters.
 SOFT. (*weeping*).   And I a ma!
DE NOGO. So young and beautiful! so folks declare of 'em,
   And no papa now to take care of 'em!
   Ah, Beauty! little did you e'er suppose
   What I should come to through your rose!
   'Twas for you I plucked this bud.
BEASTUS (*aside*). A beauty! My heart goes such a thud!
   (*To* DE NOGO.) Eh, you have a daughter?
DE NOGO.   I have, my lud!
BEASTUS. Is she beautiful?
DE NOGO.   Sublime!
BEASTUS (*placing hand on heart*).   Another thud!
   (*Aside.*) I've long sought to get married—settled down;
   But all the females in this town
   Refuse me, and my riches quite pooh-pooh,
   And then refer me to the " Zoo,"

Where, they say, " Go with all haste,
And find a partner to your taste !"
My suit is thus declined, in manner haughty,
Even by the dustman's aunt—she's over forty!
(*To* De Nogo.) I fain would wed this maiden fair !
Has she nice eyes, or long back hair,
Good teeth, straight nose, no stutter ?
Can she play—or cut thin bread and butter ?
Does she use her H's, sound her U's,
And usually mind her P's and Q's ?

De Nogo. Oh ! she's perfection !

Beastus.   Then I'll agree,
If she weds me, to let you free !

De Nogo. Ha, ha ! Saved ! rescued, I declare !   [*Picks up luggage.*
I go to fetch my daughter fair ;
She shall be yours. Please fix the wedding day !
She's only thirty thousand miles away.

Beastus (*suspiciously*). You will come back ?

Soft. *and* De Nogo.   Oh, never fear!
In six months' time you'll see us here.

Beastus. Because I'm rich !

De Nogo *to* Soft. (*aside*).   Ah ! do you hear ?

Beastus. I've fifty millions coming in a year,
Which, if I wed your girl, with you I'll share !

De Nogo *to* Soft. We'll start a villa, a carriage and a pair !

Beastus. But ere upon your journey you do start,
Pray, take some refreshment. (*Calls at side.*) What ho ! a tart,
A sugar stick, a bone to pick, or, perhaps,
You'd better ask the butler for some scraps.

[Attendant *brings on food in a tray.*

Concerted Piece, Softpate, Beastus, *and* De Nogo—*air,* " *Will you be my Hollyhock ?* " (Mohawk Minstrels).

Beastus. Now catch the telephone express,
And bring your daughter here !
She'd be enraptured, I should guess—
The pretty little dear !

De Nogo. You are so handsome, noble and true,
Her heart will pit-a-pat;
She's just the girl for such as you !

Beastus. Now, only think of that !

Chorus,

DE NOGO.   She shall be your lady fair,
         She shall be your pet, Sir!
BEASTUS.   It's very kind, I must declare,
         To think so much of me!
DE NOGO.   She shall make you buttered toast,
         Stew your joints, or boil or roast;
         Always find her at her post,
         When you come home to tea!

*[Then trio repeat Chorus, and are
dancing while Curtain falls.*

SCENE III.—INTERIOR OF BEASTUS' PALACE.

*As the Curtain rises, SIR BEASTUS, PAGES, and ATTENDANTS are
discovered holding trays with refreshments, perfumes, gloves, &c.*

Chorus of ATTENDANTS—*air, "The Keel Row."*

Here are cakes for lady fair;
     Dainty sweets; pastry, too;
Silken mittens—here's a pair,
     And a ticket for the Zoo!
Lots of pretty things—oh, yes!
     Jewellery, too, we have here,
And a book on "How to Dress
     On Seventeen-and-six a Year!"

Enter the BEAST.

BEASTUS.   Begone! you need no longer wait.   *[Exit* ATTENDANTS.
         I would for a second meditate
         Upon the progress with this Beauty I have made—
         Not very rapid, I'm sore afraid!
         And, yet, I've often wondered why
         No lady's captivated by my eye,
         My noble figure, this handsome face,
         My money, and this lovely place!
         I'm beautiful enough; accomplished, too—
         Play the piano, and tin whistle, too;

Dance a hornpipe, jump down stairs,
And recite the poem, "Three Little Bears!"
Can fence, bound, sing, or hum;
Can—but ah! my visitors come!

[*A Grand March should be played on the piano, which brings on the* ATTENDANTS, PLAINEYE, *and* PASSBYE, SOFTPATE, *and* DE NOGO *escorting* BEAUTY; *the* ATTENDANTS *range in a half-circle, and* BEAUTY *is escorted to Throne.*]

BEASTUS (*to* DE NOGO, *aside*). What does she think of me, my future pa?
How has she spoken?

DE NOGO (*dryly*). Well, she says you are
The most uncommon individual by far
She's ever met!

BEASTUS (*pleased*). Is that all true?

DE NOGO. Quite—(*aside*) I should add, outside the Zoo!

BEASTUS. Such praise is new to me—a novelty quite.
I've made an impression!

DE NOGO. I think you're right!
However, time will show.

BEASTUS. I'm sure of it!
How's her temper—any more of it?

DE NOGO. No, 'tis pretty even; but, as you're aware,
It's all due to the change of air.

[BEASTUS *getting impatient.*]

The voyage here was rather rough;
The beef, too, was very tough;
The sailors surly, the company on board—
In fact we were, Sir, most sadly bored;
The fittings bad, the cabins and the decks
Were not at all what one expects
In steamships—not wishing to be rough,
As on the subject I have said enough—
But there's little comfort and too much puff
In steamers!

BEASTUS. Come, stop that stuff!
Ho! guests, oblige me and withdraw
To the dancing room upon the second floor,
Except Miss Beauty—her papa too,
Who'll join you in a minute or two!

[*Exit* SISTERS *and* ATTENDANTS.]

Now for it! (*To* DE NOGO.) How do I look, eh?

DE NOGO. Oh! in a most captivating way!

BEASTUS. Is my collar right—my boots—my clothes?
There's no ungainly smut upon my nose?
How do you like this walk I've got? [*Struts about.*]

DE NOGO. Beautiful! Like an earwig in the mustard pot!
You're quite perfection—such a noble air!

BEASTUS. It's just a formal style.
DE NOGO (*aside*).   The performing bear!
    She'll be smitten, Sir, I guess!
BEASTUS. Then coax her into saying "yes!"
                              [*Over* DE NOGO'S *shoulder.*
    Remember, all your debts I'll pay,
    The brokers and the bailiffs send away,
    Give you money, or arrange a loan.
DE NOGO. Beauty, your Pa would speak with you alone!
                              [BEASTUS *walks up back.*
BEAUTY (*coming down*). Alone! Is it a secret, papa, dear?
DE NOGO (*looking round*). We are alone! Then lend your ear,
    And list to what I have to say.
    Sir B. would marry you to-morrow—to-day!
    Do you like him?
BEAUTY.   Don't mention that, I pray!
DE NOGO. Here's all my millions floating fast away!
    I brought you here to wed him. If you say "no!"
    Then down I on the roasting jack go;
    While, if you consent to be his wife,
    Why, I'm a millionaire for life!
BEAUTY. But he's so ugly; I couldn't bear him!
DE NOGO. Think of your father, dear, and spare him
                              [*Down on his knees.*
    From being roasted, boiled, and trussed!
BEAUTY. Is it so? Then I suppose I must!
DE NOGO. He's going to pop the question, dear!
    So, just for a second, I'll leave you here.   [*Exit* DE NOGO.
          [BEASTUS *comes down, and they look awkwardly at*
                each other; BEAUTY *hides her face behind fan.*
BEASTUS. Ahem—(*aside*) now for the winning!
    Ahem! that's usually the first beginning.
    Ahem! a—er—It's been a nice day!
BEAUTY. Er—yes—well—no—what did you say?
BEASTUS. I—er said—dash it! I've forgotten quite!
    I—said—er—it was a nasty morning to-night.   [*Confused.*
    No, that's not it—I shall in a pickle get!
BEAUTY. We've had lovely weather!
BEASTUS.   Yes! it's been very wet.
    At least, we've had no rain for a week or so—
    I mean to say, it was fine some years ago.
          [*A long pause. They are both wandering about stage*
                when they are struck with the same idea; they come
                down stage and say to each other,
    I think we shall have some rain.
BEAUTY. The usual weather topic again!
    Let's speak of something else. What do you say
    To the last new novel, song, or play—
    The latest waltz, or ball-room caper,
    Or the current story in the "Girl's own Paper?"

BEASTUS. Alas! I know not of the things you mention;
But I would crave your kind attention
To what I say—don't think me bold in now declaring
A wish that you'd be Mrs. Bearing!

BEAUTY. You talk in riddles!

BEASTUS. Then my defence—
In talking riddles, I'm talking sense.
I'm rich, have houses near and far.
Oh! will you be——

BEAUTY. I'd better look for pa!

BEASTUS. Oh! do not leave 'twixt hope and fear,
The one who loves you kneeling here;
Who lays his riches——

BEAUTY. Sir! you ought
To know with money I'm not bought!

BEASTUS. I crave forgiveness for the base suggestion,
I feel—— [*Pretends to faint.*

BEAUTY. Oh, Sir! you're ill!

BEASTUS. It's indigestion!

BEAUTY. Do you love me much?

BEASTUS. Love's not the word!
I could eat you!

BEAUTY. Oh, that's absurd!

Duet, BEASTUS *and* BEAUTY—air, " *I'll never go back any more* "
(Francis Bros. and Day).

BEASTUS. Your features, Miss, have charmed me quite,
Your style and manners too;
Your conversation does delight,
Likewise your eyes so blue!

BEAUTY. Oh, Sir! don't flatter me, I pray;
  My heart is in a twirl.
BEASTUS. Oh, be my wife! now please just say,
  My pretty English girl!

Chorus.

I'll buy you a sealskin dolman,
 I'll buy you a sealskin muff,
A beautiful hat, a tennis bat,
 Likewise a poodle rough;
I'll take you to see the Waxworks,
 My darling, whom I adore!
If you'll but agree to marry poor me,
 And never go back any more!

        [Both repeat Chorus.

BEAUTY. Since you're so kind, then " yes," I say!
BEASTUS. You will be mine! Accept my thanks, I pray!
 Oh, joy! Oh, rapture! Pretty Miss,
 Let's seal the bargain with a kiss!

   [She kisses BEASTUS, *and the light is lowered slightly*
    for a second, during which his skins fall off, and he
    appears as a PRINCE.

BEAUTY. Well, the strangest thing I've ever seen—
 It's like a pantomime!
BEASTUS.   With a transformation scene!
BEAUTY. Why, you're a prince!—at least, you look
 Like one in our picture-book,
 Which papa bought us, some years ago,
 In Ludgate Hill or Paternoster Row.
 I cannot understand!
BEASTUS.   You will anon!
 Note, when I had that bearskin on
 I was a beast—nay, don't turn pale!
 Like most beasts, I have a *tale,*
 And I will tell it—it is this:
 Until I could find out a Miss
 To love me, I should be
 A beast; but now, Miss Beauty, see!
 I've turned a Prince 'cause you loved me.
 What, ho! come hither, friends! attendants true!
 And pay your first respects to
 The Prince who will in future rule yer,
 Educate you all and school yer!

     Enter OMNES.

      *[*PRINCE *beckons* DE NOGO *to him.*

DE NOGO. Now rise, my fluctuating pecker!
 PRINCE. I make you Chancellor of the Exchequer!
 While Softpate shall be knighted,
 With an income——
 SOFT.   Thanks—delighted!

PRINCE (*to* BEAUTY). Your sisters, too, so modest and discreet,
 Shall be attendants in your suite ;
 While you—most beautiful of creatures—shall,
 With silken robes and silken fal-de-ral,
 Take morning canters with me down the Mall ;
 While your papa will very soon a dukedom get,
 And p'raps you'll be a queen, my pet !
BEAUTY. Allow me just a word, sweet Prince, to say
 To the audience—the critics of our play :
 This is a moral, somewhat newly dressed,
 But still the self-same one, you will confess :
 So by appearances don't always be guided,
 And you may (this between us is confided)
 Be called sweet pets—
DE NOGO. Clear all my debts !
BEAUTY. Alter your position—
DE NOGO. Improve your condition !
BEAUTY. Go in for a carriage—
DE NOGO. By a favourable marriage !
 Give up lodgings on the Surrey side !
BEAUTY. And be a Prince's happy bride !
 I'm so happy, and yet, alack !
 'Twas done to keep pa from——
DE NOGO (*aside*).   The roasting jack
BEAUTY (*to* PRINCE). From you, at first, I quite recoiled.
DE NOGO (*to* SOFT.). So did we from being boiled !
BEAUTY (*to* PRINCE). I own, at first, I was abashed.
DE NOGO (*to* SOFT.). So were we at being hashed !
BEAUTY. But now I think we're happy quite,
 So let us bid our friends good night !
 And with applause please kindly feast us,
 And remember the story of Beauty and Sir Beastus !

Air, " Just down the Lane " (Francis Bros. and Day).

BEAUTY. And now, dearest friends, our story is done,
  List while the tag I may sing !
 It's shown up a moral, and some little fun,
  But all will end up with a ring.
 So put on your mufflers, your scarves, and your wraps,
  And just for a second please pause !
 And give us encouragement with a few claps,
  Or, properly speaking, applause !

Chorus, OMNES.

Our story is ended, our story is done,
  And all will conclude, oh! so gay;
So now to the supper room we'll quickly run,
  In the usual juvenile way!

COURTIERS.

PLAINEYE.   PRINCE.   BEAUTY.   PASSBYE.

SOFTPATE.   DE NOGO.

Curtain.

Princess Winifred's Wish.

CHARACTERS.

PRINCESS WINIFRED.   THE LORD CHAMBERLAIN.

THE GOOD FAIRY.

COURTIERS, NOBLES, PEDESTRIANS, &c.

COSTUMES.

PRINCESS.—Hat with large feather. Gown of sateen, or lively-patterned cretonne. If an old dress is brought into use, it should be temporarily trimmed with a few yards of glacé lining, by way of a sash and huge shoulder puffs; large fan and silk handkerchief. Underneath, a ragged frock, tattered handkerchief over shoulders.

THE LORD CHAMBERLAIN.—Huge sugar-loaf hat, built out of cardboard, and trimmed with red, blue, or brown stuff; long robe—an old dressing gown would answer—with lady's fur tippet on his shoulders, high Gladstone collar, and large bow at neck; or robe could be made of cheap stuff, large circles of white cardboard up the front representing buttons; long black wand. After his exit in the first scene he should have an old patched overcoat, to slip over the robe described above, a thick comforter, old high hat; he should also have a basket of baked potatoes. When he is transformed by the FAIRY to the COURT CHAMBERLAIN, the coat, too, should be slipped off quickly at the side of the stage, to avoid a wait.

THE GOOD FAIRY.—Dress of white, pink or blue muslin, trimmed with flowers (i.e., those discarded from mamma's bonnet), silk sash, few gold ornaments, wand.

SCENERY.
SCENE I.—A ROYAL NURSERY.

Raised seat in one corner for the PRINCESS, *i.e., chair on case or box, covered with rug or fancy red quilt. If any artistic friends are available,*

D

commision them to execute some large roughly-coloured drawings, illustrating old nursery rhymes, if in a mock medæval style all the better ; these should be hung round the stage. All the toys of the household should be shown in this scene, and every COURTIER *should be in a graceful attitude, each holding a toy—one a trumpet, another a top, &c.*

SCENE II.—A FAIRY GROTTO.

Is merely to show the CHAMBERLAIN *seeking the aid of the* FAIRY *and to give opportunity for the change to Scene III. This (Scene II.) is supposed to be a fairy grotto or cave, but if a rod is fixed a short distance from the proscenium with curtain, at the close of the first scene, this can be pulled across stage. When the* FAIRY *enters, the stage should be darkened; a little blue or red magnesium light burnt here would be effective.*

SCENE III.—A STREET IN LONDON.

In this case, of course, more to be imagined than actually represented, but the door, alluded to previously, would be of great service if placed at one side of the stage and an old wall painted on some sheets of cardboard made to meet it. In front of the door should be placed a box, to represent a step, while some tattered drugget, if laid on the floor, will add to the effect.

SCENE I.—ROYAL NURSERY.

COURTIERS *discovered holding toys, and constantly bowing to* PRINCESS, *who is seated on throne, and is assuming a languid, dissatisfied air.*

Chorus of COURTIERS—*air, "Jurymen's Chorus" ("Trial by Jury")* (Chappell).
(Can be sung an octave higher.)

Does your Highness require a toy,
  In the shape of a top or triangle?
Here's a movable donkey and boy,
  A doll, a tea-set, and a mangle;
A trumpet to play you a tune,
  An organ, a spade, and a cradle;
A dresser, a bird, and a spoon,
  A soup tureen, and a ladle.

> [*Repeat last four lines, with a short dance, and
> then* COURTIERS *resume their positions.*

PRIN. (*coming down from throne*). I'm out of sorts, I don't
    deny it.
CHAMB. (*handing sweets*). A patent candy—would your Highness
    try it?
PRIN. Tut, tut! Good Sir, you risk your power
  In offering sweets when I am sour;
  So take your candy! and I'll take a view
  Of public work I have to do.
CHAMB. (*on bended knee*). Alas! alas! I grieve to say,
  There's no work to be done to-day;
  And, though it doubtless much annoys,
  I'm bound to recommend you toys.
  Your Government, your Highness, does opine,
  That you're too young.
PRIN.   I'm over nine!
  I read and write, speak languages a few, sir!
  Can sew! What would they have me do, sir?
CHAMB. That's just the point; they'd have you play,
  Like other little girls, I say.
  Why, as to public work, they said (*trembling*)—er—hum—
  They'd see about it in ten years to come.
PRIN. (*strikes* CHAMB. *with fan*). Take that! and that! and just
    discern,
  Although so young, I've fully learned
  To chastise my attendents, when e'er
  They bring bad news!
CHAMB. (*rubbing his shoulder*). Oh, dear! oh, dear!
PRIN. (*violently*). You always thwart my little plan,
  You nasty, irritating man!

> [*Goes up in a pet and sits on throne; all the
> COURTIERS are trembling with awe.*

Song, LORD CHAMBERLAIN (*rubbing shoulder*)—*air, " Dearly Beloved Brethren"* (Chas. Sheard, Holborn).

CHORUS.

I'm always in a pickle, I'm always in a stew;
My duties are so irksome, I don't know what to do.
I'd rather be a sugar-stick, or else a babe again,
I'd rather be a dustman than a Chamber-lain.

Chorus.

Pity this tottering Chamberlain! List to him, I pray;
Kindly give an ear, friends, to all he has to say.
He's snapped and he's slapped—Ah! oft and again.
Pity, oh! pity the sorrows of a Chamber-lain!

[COURTIERS *repeat Chorus.*

I'd rather be an acid drop, a biscuit, or a puff,
Some Day and Martin's blacking, a mantle, or a muff;
An icicle or bicycle, a chopper or a plane;
I'd rather be a kitten than a Chamber-lain.

[*Chorus.*

I'd rather be a bon-bon, a bloater, or a bun,
A telescope, a bit of rope, or else a bit of fun;
I'd rather be a keyhole, a spout, or window-pane,
A box of safety matches, than a Chamber-lain.

[*Chorus, with impromptu dance of* CHAMBERLAIN *and* COURTIERS.
[*The* PRINCESS *comes down from her throne, and* CHAMBERLAIN *instantly falls on his knees in a grovelling attitude before* PRINCESS.

PRIN. Come! stop this most unseemly levity!
        And I'll be brief.
CHAMB. (*trembling*).   Oh, brevity!

PRIN.   Now, just attend to what I say!
   And execute these——

CHAMB.   Be merciful, I pray!

PRIN.   Silence, Sir, or else you'll rue it!
   Now, there's a list; please first run through it.
          [*Hands* CHAMBERLAIN *a long paper.*
   I want those items, and 'tis your duty
   At once to fetch them.

CHAMB. (*aside*).   She's a beauty!

PRIN.   If not, then instantly prepare
   For torture! dungeons!

CHAMB. (*weeping*).   Is this fair?
   Such threatening gives one a shock!

PRIN.   (*furiously*). Now, read, Sir!

CHAMB. (*trembling*).   I will, like one o'clock!
   (*Aside.*) Of sympathy there's not a particle—
   (*To* PRINCESS.) Have I to get all these?

PRIN.   Yes; every article.

CHAMB. (*with handkerchief in one hand, which he occasionally ap-*
   plies to his eyes, reads). Item one:
   A cat which never scratches!
   A child who'd never play with matches!
   A schoolboy quiet as a lamb,
   And one who's never tasted jam!
   A watch that ne'er requires winding!
   A handsome book without a binding!
   A sluggard punctual to the minute!
   A schoolboy's knife without a corkscrew in it!
   A telescope of piecrust made!
   A little maiden who's afraid
   Of eating pastry—or similar comestible—
   Solely on account of being indigestible!
   A scavenger born with a silver spoon!
   And, horror! What is this?   [*Astounded.*
    [*The* COURTIERS *close round, and all shout with horror,*
        THE MOON!
    [*All the* COURTIERS *go on their knees, and the* CHAM-
    BERLAIN *falls on the ground, and weeps in the roll of*
    paper. If a little slow tragic music can be played on
    the piano at this point it will considerably add to the
    effect.

PRIN.   Yes; that's what I want, and you know my word is law!

CHAMB. I've often heard that argument before!

PRIN.   (*striking* CHAMBERLAIN *on ground*). Come! are you my
   orders going to follow up?

CHAMB. (*aside*). I wish the earth would kindly swallow up
   Poor me! Oh, dear! oh, dear! I never knew
   To such a mistress I should have to buckle to!
   (*Crying.*) Where can I get these things? I know not where!
   (*Aside.*) I'd go to Whiteley's, but they'd declare
   That, though they'd get me scavenger and spoons,
   Alas! they'd be quite out of moons.

Duet and Chorus, PRINCESS *and* CHAMBERLAIN—*air, " Up to Dick "*
(Francis Bros. and Day).

CHAMB. I really feel so very queer,
       At what I've got to do!
PRIN. Come! why, Sir, are you dawdling here?
       You must be back by two!
CHAMB. I know the cells will be my fate,
       The torture-chamber too!
PRIN. Now, bustle up, or you'll be late,
       And that you'll surely rue!

Chorus.

Then tuppence you'll give for the schoolboy,
Threepence you'll give for the cat,
Fourpence you'll give for the telescope,
Pray remember that!
Ninepence you'll give for the penknife,
Twopence you'll give for the spoon,
The rest you can keep for boarding and sleep,
While bringing us home the moon.

CHAMB. I'll promise that I'll not forget
       One item put down here.
PRIN. It's well you don't, or you will get
       A sentence from us here!
CHAMB. I'll try at every little shop,
       From Jericho to Leith.
PRIN. You'd better, or I'll quickly pop
       You in the cells beneath!
                   [*Chorus.*
[*Princess goes up to throne, attended by Maids of Honour.*

CHAMB. (*to the* COURTIERS, *who come down to receive orders*). Now
    for my journey to make preparation:
    Firstly, some eatables—my one consolation;
    It buoys me up—I always find it meet,
    When coldly treated, to get something to eat.
    John, fetch my carriage rug—my hat-box, too!
    James, bring me a warming pan or two!

> [*The Courtiers are bringing the articles, and
> placing them all round* CHAMBERLAIN.

    Simon—my eyeglass, a toothpick, a taper;
    Some stationery, pens, ink, and paper!
    William—my note-book; some salmon fried,
    With several volumes of Bradshaw's Guide!
    Arthur—my macintosh, and mind you brush it!
    Also my smoking cap—pray, don't crush it!
    My water-jug, my brush and comb,
    My favourite ballad—"Home! Sweet Home!"
    Samuel—my overcoat, and shaving pot,
    My fishing rod; and that's the lot!
COURTIER. Is that all you want, good Master?
CHAMB. No—several yards of Poor Man's Plaster,
    By the Faculty highly recommended.
PRIN. I trust, Sir, now your list is ended?
CHAMB. Oh! yes, your Highness, these are but a trifling few,
    Considering what I've to go through.
    Come! help me with my luggage, fellahs;
    Pray, where are now my umbrellas?

> [*The* COURTIERS *all swarm round him, and pile rugs,
> coats, scarfs, and mufflers on* CHAMBERLAIN. *They
> load him with parcels and articles, and the comic
> business must be kept up by his constantly dropping
> and scattering them about.*

PRIN. Now, try at every little shop
    Up Burlington Arcade!
CHAMB. My heart goes flippity-flippity-flop!
    I'm fainting, I'm afraid!
OMNES. And don't forget the tabby cat,
    The scavenger and spoon;
    The telescope—pray think of that.
    And don't forget the Moon!

> [*Slowly, with a tragic air; all bowing low.*

> [*While this last verse is being sung all the
> COURTIERS are swarming round* CHAMBER-
> LAIN *and piling his parcels, &c., on him as
> the Curtain is drawn.*

SCENE II.—THE FAIRY GROTTO.

Stage slightly dark. While this scene is on, the back one should be proceeded with. (See instructions at commencement.)

Enter the GOOD FAIRY. *As soon as she reaches the middle of the stage a violent knocking is heard, and* CHAMBERLAIN *rushes in, piled up with rugs, coats, and parcels, &c., which he, of course, constantly drops. Directly he catches sight of the* FAIRY, *he goes through a series of pantomimic bows.*

FAIRY. Good evening, noble Sir! Pray, why this visit?

                          [CHAMBERLAIN *weeps.*

Dear me! some private sorrow! Pray, what is it?
You're muffled up; are you a friend or foe-man?
Perhaps the tax collector?

CHAMB. (*Pointing to his wardrobe*).   No! Old Clo' Man!
Or, rather, Chamberlain—an office, which, alas!
That after Friday morning to another one will pass;
While I in dungeon dismal, drear, and damp,
Will perish!

FAIRY (*aside*).   I suppose, then, he's a scamp!

CHAMB. So, seeing on your door-plate, down below,
That you assisted mortals when they're so
Weighed down with grief, I thought I'd just inquire
Your price for dragging from the mire
Of royal affairs, the man who stands before you now?

FAIRY. This seems to be an urgent case.

CHAMB.   It is, I vow!
It is my mistress, the noble Princess, who
Continually puts one in the worst of stew!
In fact, I'm ordered by to-morrow afternoon!
To bring her, for a plaything, a nice full moon!
If not, they'll pack me by the late express
To the deepest dungeon in Dungeness.

FAIRY. I take no cash for what I do;
I look upon it as a duty too.

CHAMB. (*rubbing his hands joyfully.*) I see at last of hope a gleam.
Is it a reality or a dream?
How will you manage it?

FAIRY.   Leave that to me.
And, to start with—Presto! See!

      [*She waves her wand and the stage darkens; this gives
           an opportunity for the* PRINCESS *to get on the stage,
           a few inches from the left side. The lights are raised,
           and she is discovered standing as still and lifeless as
           possible.* CHAMBERLAIN *is in the greatest confusion.*

CHAMB. (*trembling*). Her Highness! and I'm discovered—brought
      to book!

FAIRY. You've nought to fear! she cannot see you. Look!
Now, sister fairies, round me range
While I propel this mystic change!

Lend me your aid ; for now I would
Propel a change, p'raps for the good.
A Princess Royal of high degree
A tinge of bitter life shall see ;
Shall taste the cup of sorrow, then
Ask aid, in vain, from heartless men—
A struggling bark, on angry wave,
An outcast on the London pave ;
Unheeded, hungry, weary too.   [*Waves her wand.*
A London waif I change thee to !

> [*Here the lights must be lowered for a second, to enable*
> PRINCESS *to slip off her dress, and pass it quickly to*
> *some one ready to take it at the side. The light is*
> *raised as she is standing in the same position.*
> *The second dress should be as ragged as possible,*
> *and she should have some flowers in her hand, and some*
> *in an old basket.*

Bubble, bubble, joy or trouble !
 Princess proud, His Grace forlorn!
Act your parts as Fate decrees them !
 Presto ! magic ! both begone!

> [*The* FAIRY *waves her wand while the Curtain is slowly*
> *pulled on one side, and the* PRINCESS *is discovered*
> *sitting on the step.*

       [*Exit* FAIRY, *Right entrance.*

SCENE III.—A LONDON STREET.

Supposed to be winter. Small scraps of white paper can be scattered
about the floor, and all the characters should have small pieces of white
wool stuck over their costumes, especially on their hats and shoulders.
PEDESTRIANS *must be constantly hurrying across the stage, muffled up*
to convey an idea of extreme cold. The PRINCESS *endeavours to sell*
her flowers to the passers-by, but is gruffly repulsed, and ordered to
get out of the way.

PRIN. Alas ! how cold it is ! I feel so weary.
   And this is London, so chill and dreary !
   And yet somewhere I have been told
   That London's streets were paved with gold !
   I've looked in vain for pavement so rare,
   But found not gold, nor even coppers, there.
   Who will a rose or violet buy ?
   Alas ! no one answers to that cry.
   I feel so hungry, broken-hearted, too !
   If no luck comes whatever shall I do ?

       [*A* PEDESTRIAN *comes quickly across.*

Here, Sir ! won't you buy a violet or a rose ?
(*Looking after him.*) He's got no use for flowers, I suppose.

It's getting dark; the stars begin to peep!
That just reminds me—wherever shall I sleep?
Ah, sleep's a comfort! 'Tis then I seem
To have such dinners, in a dream!
How cold it is! Why, I declare!
A doorway! I'll huddle up in there.   [*Sits in doorway.*
How sleepy I feel! Oh, dear! oh, dear!
I'll rest a little while down here.
  [*Sinks down on doorstep. A crowd begins to congregate*
   round her; they look at her for a few minutes, then go
   off one by one.

FIRST PED. (*to* SECOND DITTO). She seems in a very, very weak
  condition.   [*Drawing penny from his pocket.*
I'll give a pen—— (*suspiciously*); but p'raps it's imposition!
She's very likely shamming, might and main,
So go you to my pocket, little penny, once again!
   [*Pockets the penny, and exit with* PEDESTRIAN No. 2.

Enter PEDESTRIAN No. 3. *Goes up to the* PRINCESS.

Dear, dear! how sad! Why I'm afraid
The cold will kill this little flower maid!
Such poverty distresses much my mind.
       [*Puts his hand in his pocket.*
Here's sixpence for—— (*feels in his pocket, and his face
  undergoes contortions of horror*)—I've left my purse
  behind!
   [*Exit in a hurry. Stage slightly darker.*

Enter CHAMBERLAIN (*in costume previously described*). *He carries a
  basket of baked potatoes, looking very cold.*

CHAMB. Baked 'taters! all hot and floury! and all!
That's what I now continually call.
But customers are scarce, its quite appalling!
I am afraid this is a sorry calling;
The trade in my idea's a wreck,
Like Cornish tin mines, a wretched spec!
(*Cries out.*) All hot and floury! Won't you buy?
I get quite hoarse with my continual cry,
And tired with my never-ceasing round,
Through a hundred streets. Now, I'll be bound——
      [*Sees* PRINCESS *lying on doorstep.*
Hullo! what's this? A flower girl! and in distress!
Suffering from a complaint one easily can guess.
Prescription—a good dinner, warmth (things unknown to
  the poor);
Treatment—the mixture taken as before.
(*Rubbing her hands.*) She's terribly cold. Ah! a good
  idea!   [*Puts her hands on his basket.*
Now, little sufferer, just lay your hands on here.
PRIN. (*waking*). How warm it is! I cannot understand!
(*Rubbing her eyes.*) Where am I?
CHAMB.   In baked-potato land.

[Taking out a hot potato and breaking it.

There's a beauty! Eat that now, while it's hot,
And after you can have some more. I've such a lot!

PRIN. (*eating ravenously*). Oh! this is lovely! I feel so much
    stronger;
I think I should have died if I'd fasted any longer.

CHAMB. Where do you live when you're at home, my little lass?

PRIN. Where do I live? I have no home, alas!
No friends; no one who's ever smiled on me but you.

[Embraces him.

CHAMB. It's wonderful, now, what a baked potato can just do!
No home! no friends! A dreary situation, pheu!
But, come! cheer up, my darling, I'll see what I can do.
My little lot I'll share, and you shall be my guest;
It isn't much to offer, but perhaps it's for the best.
Henceforth of my potatoes I shall be the taker,

PRIN. And I——

CHAMB.   Give up the flower trade and be my baker.

PRIN. How can I thank you, oh, kind Sir! I——

[Sinks down in a swoon.

CHAMB. (*bending over her*). Poor little weakling! No longer shall
    you stay
Out in this cold; but, come what may,
I'll see you housed this very day!

*[Lifts her from the ground, and is about to carry her off
the stage, when GOOD FAIRY enters with all the
COURTIERS, dressed as in Scene I. The stage is
darkened on the entrance of FAIRY, giving opportunity
for change of the two costumes. PRINCESS and
CHAMBERLAIN stand perfectly still until the FAIRY
changes them.*

FAIRY. I'm glad to see my little plan
Successfully finished, as it so began.
Like other works in my dominion,
It shows a moral—such is my opinion—
That little folks may well take into mind,
And—there, but you are not inclined
To listen to the lecture in your present frame of mind!
Awake, Princess! I charge thee, move
From out your present gutter groove!
Discard your old and tattered dress,
And, Presto! change thee to a fair Princess!

[The old gown is slipped off and the lights are raised.

PRIN. Where have I been? Perhaps I'm dreaming, and
I'm wandering in some sleepy land! *[Feels the stage.*
Yet no! This cold damp stone—there is a lamp-post, too!
This is not dreamland I have journeyed to!

[Catches sight of the basket of flowers.

I now remember I was a little gutter maiden,
Weary, broken-hearted, and with sorrow laden.

I should have starved, I know it well,
When, in a kind of stupor, fell
Upon the threshold of that doorway there,
Then I awoke, and oh! some stranger blessed
Restored me.

FAIRY.   Yes, Princess, we know the rest.

PRIN. Princess! you call me, lady—why Princess?

                                        [*Looks at her dress.*

Ah! this ring—these jewels—this dress—
Recalls the past—it flits before my eyes—yes!

                                        [*Going on her knees.*

I was a very naughty, naughty Princess.
I was capricious, on a certain afternoon,
And ordered my poor Chamberlain to go and fetch the moon;
If he disobeyed, I harshly told him pat
He'd be imprisoned.

CHAMB. (*perfectly still*).   I didn't much like that!

PRIN. (*weeping*). It rankles in my heart—that treatment so severe.
Alas! where is he now?

FAIRY.   He is here.

PRIN. Here, you say!   I cannot see him, lady, fair!

            [*Sees* CHAMBERLAIN, *who remains like a statue.*

But there's my dear restorer over there!

                                        [*Kneels at his feet.*

Oh, let me thank—why don't you move?   You seem
Just like a statue in a dream!
Pray, lady, how is this he does not greet me?
(*Weeping.*) Oh! after all your kindness, is this the way to
    treat me?

FAIRY. You are confused.   Allow me to explain,
And show you a transformation once again!
This baked-potato seller, who treated you with care,
Was none other than the Chamberlain who's standing over
    there!
When suffering from treatment you've alluded to before,
He happened to catch sight of the plate upon my door;
He sought my aid, in fact we had a consultation—
It ended in a double transformation:
You to a flower girl, sad at heart and weary,
Him to a baked-potato seller cheery.
Recall his kindness in tending so to you—
Recall how noble——

PRIN.   I do—I do!
I will seek forgiveness at his hands!

FAIRY. I prithee not as he at present stands!
For hubble, bubble, joy and gladness once again!

        [*The stage is darkened for an instant to allow change of
            dress, and the* PRINCESS *and* CHAMBERLAIN *clasp
            hands.*

CHAMB. My Princess!

PRIN.   My Chamberlain!

Now let me on my bended knee
Seek forgiveness, Sir, from thee,
For having treated you so badly!

CHAMB. (*affected*). I do, your Highness—gladly, gladly!
PRIN. No longer will you find me in any way refractory.
FAIRY. I think the whole affair's been concluded satisfactory.
PRIN. As a baked potato saved me, I hereby declare
I'll always have a little placed upon our bill of fare.
(*Looks round.*) What ho! my noble Courtiers! let me
shake each by the hand!

[*Shakes hands all round.*

While you, my dear old Chamberlain, will entertain the
band—
In fact, we'll have a supper that will far outshine
Anything attempted in the brilliant supper line;
And you, sweet Fairy, you're cordially invited
To stay a fortnight with us.

FAIRY.   I shall be delighted
I might as well, my dear Princess, inform you, by the way,
That from your noble palace we're ten thousand miles
away!

[*They all commence looking about them.*

PRIN. Can you take us home, then, Fairy, dear?
Or, better, change the scene, as you appear
To have such sway o'er things like these—
Pray, just oblige us, Fairy, please!
FAIRY. I will. Hey, Presto!—but on consideration,
As our play is near its termination,
I'll wait until the curtain's down,
And then we'll journey to your town.

Duet, PRINCESS *and* CAAMBERLAIN—air, "*Another Jolly Row Down-
stairs*" (Francis Bros. and Day).

PRIN.   We'll be so happy now,
                         No bickering, I vow!
CHAMB.   Farewell, all worries and all cares;
                         We'll live a jolly life,
                         No quarrelling or strife,
                And no nasty rows downstairs!

The COURTIERS *dance a breakdown, and Curtain falls on characters*
in the following position:

                         COURTIERS.
      FAIRY.   CHAMBERLAIN.   PRINCESS.

A Winter's Day Dream.

CHARACTERS.

FAIRY OF THE GOLDEN DELL ⎫
FAIRY INDUSTRIA................. ⎬ Immortals.
THE OGRE SLOTH................. ⎭

FAIRY OFFICER................... ⎫
FLORRIE .... ⎬ Mortals.
PATTIE .... ⎭

FAYS, ATTENDANTS TO THE OGRE.

COSTUMES.

FLORRIE AND PATTIE.—Ordinary every-day dress.

FAIRY INDUSTRIA.—Similar costume, but should have a necklace of small reels of cotton, while at her side should be hung a dustpan and little toy broom. A little satchel suspended from her sash should have needlework; her attendants should also have some mark of industry to carry in their hands, such as brooms, dustpans, rolling pins, &c.

THE OGRE SLOTH.—A costume made to look as dirty and dilapidated as possible; a long wig, which could be very well made from an old muff or mat; and a badly-fitting coat, torn to tatters, with trousers or knickerbockers of any coloured material, all jagged at the bottoms and begrimed with dirt. The Ogre's face should be dirty, while his movements should be of the shambling and lazy order. The Ogre's minions should be modelled after their master, as far as possible.

SCENERY.

SCENE I.—ORDINARY DRAWING ROOM.

With three hassocks or chairs in a prominent position.

SCENE II.—INDUSTRIA.

A large pair of curtains hung at the back, just to give a slight distinction from previous scene, is all that is necessary, but stools or chairs should be placed in a half-circle round stage (à la Christy Minstrel entertainment), which are occupied by FAIRY INDUSTRIA'S *attendants, busy with some piece of work, one mending clothes, another boots, a third a hat. The* FAIRY *occupies a throne in the centre, and Characters should enter and exit from either right or left.*

SCENE. III.—THE REGION OF SLOTHDUM.

Tattered sacking strewn about the floor, and old drugget hung round the walls. All the attendants are reclining in a lazy position round their Chief, who is lolling in the centre of the stage. A pair of curtains should be fixed at the front of the stage, and should be on a rod, to avoid a wait in closing a scene.

——

SCENE I.—ORDINARY DRAWING ROOM.

FLORRIE *and* PATTIE *discovered. Stage dark.* (*A magnesium light burnt here would look very pretty.*) *One is sitting on a chair looking at a picture book, while the other is at her feet with a toy or doll as the scene opens. The following Chorus is sung very softly by the* FAIRIES *outside, accompanied, if possible, on the piano :*

Air, " Somebody Whispered so sweetly" (Francis Bros. and Day).

Darkness ends the day so dreary,
　　Dustman's coming quickly here!
Children tired, worn out, weary,
　　He will catch you, never fear!

　　　　　　　[*The* CHILDREN, *while the song is
　　　　　　　　being sung, gradually fall asleep.*

Now the stars above are peeping,
　　Journey to the dreamy land;
Hush! they're sleeping, sleeping, sleeping!
　　Haste thee, haste, my fairy band!

　　　　　　　[*This is gradually lowered until the
　　　　　　　　voices become almost indistinct.*

Chorus of OGRES.

Should be sung in a low gruff voice at side of stage.

Now, my trusty Ogres true,
    When, from daylight's searching glare,
We, all safe, secure too,
    Draw some victims to our snare.
Act with stealth, premeditation,
    Lure them to the slothful cave,
Overcome their hesitation!
    Come, each true and trusty slave!

[*At the close of this Chorus a sentimental air should be
played softly on the piano, to bring on* FAIRY INDUS-
TRIA, *who enters from the right, and beckons* FLORRIE
*to follow her, and exits. The same course is followed
by the* OGRE SLOTH, *who beckons* PATTIE *to follow
him; all this being simply* ballet d'action, *the music
will be all the more appropriate. On the exit of the*
OGRE *the stage curtains are drawn, and the arrangement of Scene II. proceeded with, according to the
directions previously given, with as much dispatch as
possible, so as to avoid a wait.*

SCENE II.—INDUSTRIA.

Chorus, INDUSTRIA'S FAIRIES—*air, "Jolly as a Sandboy"* (Francis
Bros. and Day).

We're jolly here as sandboys,
    And happy as your kings,
When stitching here so gaily,
    And patching up old things!
We never think of lounging,
    We've got beyond that far,
And when we have fresh work to do,
    We laugh, ha, ha! ha, ha!

E

IND. (*bringing out note book*). Now let's review our duties for to-day.
   Please stop work for just a second, I pray !
   Firstly, note the progress we have made ;
   Things are rather dull, I am afraid ;
   But there, our headway's slow, but steady !

     Enter an ATTENDANT.

ATTEND. Please, Marm, the prisoners are ready !
FAIRY. Good !—bring them up in strict rotation
          [*Exit* ATTENDANT.

   To undergo examination ;
   And while upon the bench I'm sitting,
   I'll just resume my piece of knitting.
     [*The* FAIRIES *now bring up their work for the
      Chief's inspection ; they follow each other.*

1ST FAIRY (*showing work*).   Have I made this gusset neatly ?
 IND. Oh, you've done it, sister, sweetly !
2ND FAIRY. Do you like this little bonnet ?
 IND. It's beautiful, I'm sure !
 FAIRY. Do you like my hem upon this stuff ?
 FAIRY. Pray is this pie-crust light enough ?
   Are ribbons suited to this muff ?
 IND. They're beautiful, I'm sure !
FAIRIES. Is this crochet to your liking ?
 IND. Yes, I think it's very striking.
FAIRIES. Is this pattern worked out neatly ?
 IND. Beautiful, I'm sure !
FAIRIES. Do you like this kettle-holder ?
 IND. Well, the hemming might be bolder.
FAIRIES. Is this tatting to your liking ?
 IND. Beautiful, I'm sure !

   [*A cry is heard without, and all the* FAIRIES *look
    off the stage ; the stage is slightly darkened.*

   Who comes, who comes ?   Pray let me know !
   Is it a friend, or is it a foe ?
   And yet I know that voice so well—
   The lovely Fairy of the Golden Dell !

   [*Enter a* FAIRY OF THE GOLDEN DELL, *carrying*
    FLORRIE, *who is fast asleep. All* INDUSTRIA'S
    ATTENDANTS *are eagerly scanning the child, who is
    laid down on a pallet while the* FAIRIES *all kneel
    around her.*

 IND. Come, good sister, some explanation
   Of this, your very last sensation !
   A pretty child, I must confess !
   And shows us plainly by her dress
   Her rank is high ; but sister, pray,
   Tell how you came with her—kindly say !
FAIRY. List ! and I will tell you, sister dear,
   How I came with this little creature here.

'Twas hard by, in the dismal glen,
Where Sloth and all his creeping men
For victims make nightly raid.

IND. With some success, I'm sore afraid!

FAIRY. 'Twas twilight, and I sat musing in my grotto,
Thinking out some Christmas bon-bon motto
(Having been so ordered by Parkins and Gotto),
When suddenly I saw——

OMNES. What!

FAIRY. Two children, with the Ogre and his lot—
The Ogres using artifices and wiles,
All blandishment, civility, and smiles,
While now and then a sweet or two they gave,
As they slyly wandered to their cave.
Oh! how my heart bled at their fate!
I thought of you, but all too late;
I struggled with them, took this little maid;
The other they have taken, I am much afraid.
Most of my fairy power's gone, as I have stated,
I'm retired now—

IND. And superannuated.
But let me thank you with my heart,
For having acted so noble a part!
Henceforth this little child shall be our care.
A sojourn in Industria will help her, I declare,
In going through the world of trouble, joy, and sorrow,
Of dirty grates, water rates, call again to-morrow!
Of boots with broken laces, chapped hands and faces,
Of naughty boys who make a noise, also grimaces.
Another duty we'll not overlook,
And that to bring the Ogres right to book,
Rescue the other girls from Slothdum's clutch—

[ATTENDANT *pops her head in at the door.*

ATTEND. The prisoners are ready, Marm.

IND. I thought as much.
But see, the child is waking, see!   [FLORRIE *wakes up.*

FLO. (*looking round*). Well! wherever can I be?
This isn't our parlour, and, I am sure
It's not our nursery—there's no litter on the floor;
And where is nurse? Jack would call this "rummy;"
And where's old Flo, and where is mummy?
And, best of all, where is this?

IND. Industria, my little miss.

FLO. Industria! I cannot understand,
Miss Limber never speaks of such a land;
I've heard of India, France, and Spain,
Australia, and Hampstead, over and over again;
But Industria, wherever can it be?
It's not on our map. I'll go and see.
But I forgot, we're miles and miles away.
Who's brought me here, and what's to-day?

IND. I'll explain quite fully in a minute;
    And now for our trial, we'll please begin it!
      [*The* FAIRIES *resume their places, and sing the chorus,*
        "*We're jolly here as Sandboys,*" *&c.* TWO FAIRY
        OFFICERS *bring on a* SCHOOLBOY *with large pinafore,*
        and a dunce's cap; he looks very awkward and abashed.

IND. Pray, explain the charge!

FAIRY OF. This is a schoolboy; hear me, pray—
    A case requiring prompt attention—
    A deeply-rooted love of play,
    And other painful things to mention.
    His face is rarely ever clean,
    His hair a comb is sadly lacking;
    A brush his coat has never seen,
    His boots are quite unknown to blacking.

OMNES.   Oh, yes! oh, yes! we quite agree
        A very urgent case we see.

FAIRY OF. He's always last to enter school,
    And then with gapes, and nods, and yawning;
    And lately he has made a rule,
    To give up washing in the morning.
    While just to mention education,
    He's mastered half the A B C;
    And so I have no hesitation
    In bringing up this case to thee.

OMNES.   Oh yes! oh yes! we quite agree
        A very urgent case we see.

IND. Pray, good attendants, just observe!
    The sentence of the Court for the present I'll reserve.
    Stand this youth aside, my officer true,
    And bring up your prisoner Number Two.
      [*The* TWO FAIRIES *exit, and enter holding a sleepy*
        looking SHOP BOY *with basket, &c.*

FAIRY OF. An errand boy of habits lazy;
    A very shocking case, you'll say!
    His conduct drives his master crazy,
    By loitering so on the way.
    When sent with tea, or soap, or jumbles,
    He'll play at marbles half the day;
    With naughty boys he jumps and tumbles,
    In quite an acrobatic way.

OMNES.   Oh yes! oh yes! we quite agree
        A very urgent case we see.

FAIRY OF. When sent with Mrs. Jones' pot-herbs,
    He'll sometimes take it in his head
    To wander to some distant suburbs,
    And fish for sticklebacks instead.
    When sent with Mr. Jones' ointment,
    Who suffers sorely from the gout,
    With little boys he'll make appointment
    To rake some little bird nests out.

OMNES. Oh yes! oh yes! we quite agree
A very urgent case we see.

[INDUSTRIA *waves her wand, and the* ERRAND BOY *is delivered into the hands of the* FAIRIES, *while the* OFFICERS *exit and enter with a little* SERVANT GIRL, *extremely dirty, old print dress and slipshod shoes; she should have a brush and dust pan, she appears very sulky when brought in, and eyes the* FAIRIES *with anything but friendly glances.*

FAIRY OF. A hopeless case, I am afraid;
Important in the household matters;
A most untidy servant maid,
A very bunch of rags and tatters!
She never leaves her bed till ten;
Her face, you see, she seldom washes;
Her kitchen is an awful den;   [*Points to* SERVANT'S *feet.*
She's partial, too, to old goloshes.

OMNES. Oh, yes! oh, yes! we quite agree
A very urgent case we see.

IND. Of hope, I'm glad to say, there are some traces
At present gleaming through these urgent cases;
The sentence shall be light, so prisoners understand
You'll pass three months in this Industria land!

                         [*Turning to* FLORRIE.

I trust you know our object better, dear.
FLOR. As our lecturer says: The object's very clear.
You're all so very good, and I am sure
I begin to like you more and more.
May I stay? you're such nice people here:
But Mamma, she'll scold me so, I fear!
IND. Don't fear on that account, my dear.
FLOR. But where's my sister, is she here?
IND. Alas! the child awakens me to duty,
To rescue Slothdum's recent booty.
Come, good Fairies, haste thee, pray,
And make for Slothdum, without delay!

      [*All the* FAIRIES *start up and are marching out as the curtain falls, singing the following*:

Rub, rub, rub, no time we lose;
Brush, brush, brush up all the shoes,
            &c., &c.

SCENE III.—SLOTHDUM.

Stage dark as the curtain rises. Some slow sombre music would prove effective; a red magnesium light would also add to the scene.

SLOTH. (*to* ATTENDANT). How goes our prisoner?—dost thou know?
Does she sleep?
ATTEND.   Aye, surely so!

SLOTH. How goes the time? (*Looks at watch.*) Why, by my power!
We're close upon the magic hour,
When we can bind, as fast as Judson's Gum,
All those who in our power come!
Once past that hour (*savagely*)—abomination!—
Our one peg is fascination.
So wake my trusty Ogres, true!

> [*Kicks each one ; they rise dazed.*

And see what good you all can do
In winning to our cause, I say,
This little girl we caught to-day!

OGRES.   Aye! Aye!

> [*They all go to sleep again.*

SLOTH (*warmly*).   I want you now, you heard me say before!
Your " Aye, Aye," is'nt worth a straw.
(*Looks round.*)   And yet, how beautifully my system works!
They're all perfection as to shirks.
It pleases me to shield them when
They're such a lazy set of men ;
So noble, dirty, sleepy, true,
There's nothing that they like to do!

> [*A toll of a bell is heard.*

The very hour striking pat !   [*Kicks the* OGRES *again.*
Awake! Take that, and that, and that!
Now bear attention, if you can keep awake,
And listen to the statement I'm about to make :
See ! I draw upon the floor
The magic circles—you've seen it done before.

> [*Draws a circle.*

Our victim must be lured there,
But by persuasion, so take care
To use no kind of manual force,
Or you will rue it !

OGRES.   We shall, of course !

SLOTH. Once in the circle—you know the rest—
Henceforth she's one of us.   Now do your best !
While your reward, if once she's here,   [*Pointing to circle.*
Will be a bath once, instead of twice a year.
No change of linen for three years at least,
And then, by way of sumptuous feast,
A three months' sleep without awaking,
Except the morning milk to take in,
The butter, watercress, and bread,
Hot rolls, and then, you " rolls " again to bed.

OGRES. Here, here !   We wait to do our duty.

SLOTH. 'Tis well. (*Calling in a winning voice.*) Pattie, come here,
my beauty!

> [*Enter* PATTIE, *crying.   She looks round, very much surprised, and all the* OGRES *begin bowing and wheeling about in the most fascinating manner.*

PAT. Wherever am I ?   What a dirty place!   [*Looks at* SLOTH.
And hasn't he an awful face !
Please, Sir, I've lost my way !
SLOTH.   Too true !
And I've found thee.
PAT.   How good of you !
Am I far from home ?
SLOTH.   'Tis so, I fear !
PAT. Many miles ?
SLOTH.   Several from here.
PAT. Mamma will be in such a fuss !
Are there no trains, or omnibus ?
SLOTH. Alas, no ! in this lone solitary spot,
An omnibus we haven't got ;
The roads are now in such a state
That we invite you here to wait,
And though our style may be confusing,
You'll find that it's at least amusing.
PAT. Oh, thanks ! but you're so dirty—quite appalling !
SLOTH. Don't call us names—it is our *calling.*
PAT. Pray, do you ever wash, or comb your tresses ?
I've never been so black as you !
SLOTH. (*pretending to cry*).   Such talk distresses
Him who has to bear the weight
Of such tresses on his pate !
We never wash, or comb, or scent,
Because—because—aye, there's the rub !—
If done to-day, then, to your sorrow,
You'll find it just as bad to-morrow ;
Thus, then, exertion's thrown away.
PAT. It's very truthful what you say,
To be like you would be great fun.
SLOTH. (*pleased*) It would, it would ! pray, take a bun.
PAT. Thanks, I'm hungry.
SLOTH.   Then have another one.
                                        [*Hands bun.*

(*Aside to* OGRES.)   The magic time is quickly waning ;
Our object we must quick be gaining.
                        [*Puts a toy in centre of magic circle.*

PAT. Oh ! what is that ? a dolly or a top ?
SLOTH. No ! A foreign kind of lollipop ;
Tis yours, my pet !
             [PATTIE *looks at it, then goes to throne and nestles down.*
PAT.   Please, bring it here !
SLOTH. No ! you must fetch it, little dear.
PAT. I'm very cosy up here coiled ;
I'm too tired !
OGRES.   And we are foiled !
SLOTH (*aside*).   Not so fast ! use all persuasion, pray,
And try it in a more attractive way !

Chorus of OGRES—*air*, "*Where the Simple Daisies grow*."

[*They all kneel before* PATTIE.

Oh! hear our song, sweet little maiden,
    And list to what we ask of thee!
We come with lots of dainties laden—
    A pretty present you will see.
We would you join our joyful set here,
    For your sweet company we yearn;
In dirt and rags you would look prettier!
    Now, hear what we give in return.

Your life would be composed of play,
    All kinds of lessons you could shirk,
You'd lay abed the livelong day,
    And never, never, mention work.
When winter comes, so cold and dreary,
    And if the frost at all you dread,
Why, then the little maiden dreary,
    Can have her breakfast brought in bed!

PAT. That would be nice, would'nt it!
SLOTH.   Yes.
PAT. No nasty needlework!
SLOTH.   And no governess!
PAT. No English History!
SLOTH.   Nor Mavor's spelling.
PAT. No tell tales!
SLOTH.   There's no telling.
PAT. No composition?
SLOTH.   Nor summing up?
PAT. Then I'll join you!
SLOTH (*aside to* OGRES).   Prepare—she's coming up!
PAT. (*coming just outside circle*). This is the ring!
SLOTH.   It is, my dear.
PAT. And I have just to step in here,
    And this chalk line will bring about
    The changes which you've sung about!
SLOTH (*aside*). The fatal hour's near at hand!
    There's no deception, you will understand.
PAT. There's no harm in it?

SLOTH. Oh, no! it's strictly fair.
The ring's quite good—it's all marked there!
PAT. Then here goes—
SLOTH. (*anxiously*). Be quick, I pray!
PAT. Which foot first?
IND. (*outside*). Stay! I charge thee, stay!

Enter INDUSTRIA *with* FAIRIES, *&c.;* FLORRIE *and* PATTIE *embrace each other, and the* PRISONERS *in the first scene are now very busy.*

SLOTH. Foiled! Defeated! Baffled! Done!
The fatal hour's struck! (INDUSTRIA *strikes him with her wand.*) Just struck one!
IND. So this is how you lure and entice
Your victims—you are very, very nice!
By magic circles promising so grand
The products of your lazy land!
I was in time, I'm proud to say,
And so it proved to your dismay;
But, coming to the point, I cannot demolish you quite,
But as a sweet reminder of to-night,
Supposing for a year or so
You and your Ogres to Industria go.
SLOTH *and* OGRES. Oh! spare us, Oh!
IND. That is my solemn sentence; so prepare
For work, early rising, and fresh air!
In the fields you will have to work again,
And gather corn—that will go against your *grain.*
But what you'll suffer most—pray, stop this yawning—
You'll have to wash your faces every morning.
SLOTH (*on knees*). What! wash our faces once a day?
Oh! Fairy, show some mercy, pray!
Is there no forbearance—not a gleam of hope?
IND. None. Prisoners, prepare for soap!
FLO. *and* PAT. When can we see mamma, Fairy dear?
IND. Oh, shortly, she's but a little way from here;
At present you're in dreamland, but it seems
There's plenty of good lessons learnt in dreams.
So tell your ma, your pa, and grandmother as well,
What strange adventures one night befel
Two little maidens in a dreamy land,
Industria and Slothdum!
FLO. *and* PAT. We understand.
IND. How one knows dearly to her cost
How near in Slothdum she was lost,
But by Industria was saved, and now
She'll never journey there again.
PAT. I won't, I vow!
IND. So all ends " merrily as a marriage bell."
[*Winks to* OGRE.
Even there may be hope here—who can tell?
But come, we've got to journey through the town,
So, papa, kindly ring the curtain down!

Chorus, OMNES—*air, " Oh, very well, Mary Ann."*

So now we all will toddle to Industriah;
We've had enough of Slothdum, tra-la-la-la-la,
We'll show these lazy people how clean we are,
Tra-la-la, tra-la-la, la-la-la !

Curtain.

A Case of Toys.

DRAMATIS PERSONÆ.

FAIRY THINKOFIT...Under an engagement to the Lowther Arcadians.
FLISSY ....An Aristocratic Eight-year-older.
FLOSSY ....An Aristocratic Nine-year-older.
SARAH GIBLEY ......A London Waif.
POLLY ....Her Sister.

The following characters may be introduced, *ad. lib.*: Red Riding Hood; Cinderella; Simple Simon; Jack Horner; Boy Blue; Little Bo-peep; Baby Bunting; Farmer's Boy; Mary, Mary, quite contrary; Queen of Hearts; Knave of Hearts, &c.

ACT I.

SCENE.—SANCTUM OF THE GOOD FAIRY THINKOFIT.

Ordinary room, in general disorder, picture books, toys, &c., strewn about the floor; table covered with toys, paint boxes, cosaques; all the old toys of the household can be brought into use in this scene. At the back of the stage should be fixed a pair of curtains, through which the characters should make their exits and entrances. The FAIRY is the eldest character in the play, and should be represented by a young girl from 14 to 16, or as near that age as possible. As the scene opens (folding doors, or curtains, as arranged) she leans meditatively on the table, then opens one or two letters, and flings them languidly aside. An overture on the piano may be introduced, consisting of some well-known nursery tunes.

FAIRY. Alas! no fresh idea does flit across my brain:
      Though I have tried to think, with might and main,

Of something fresh to please the girls and boys—
A wonder—in the way of toys!
My past conceptions—useful, that is clear—
Have all received their moulding here.
Although on hand I have a heap,
The mouldy ones go very cheap.
But let me think o'er some of my successes!
This doll (*takes up doll*), to wit, with flaxen tresses,
Was of mine a happy notion,
Gaining for me quick promotion;
As minions of each toy arcade
For ever after sought my aid.
My list of novelties, I say,
Is quite extensive in its way;
I've made a list, and, if you've no objection,
I'll give you just a short selection.

Song—air, Chorus of " Half-a-dozen Beaux."

A monkey on a little stick,
    A novel spade and pail,
A strutting little peacock,
    With an ever-spreading tail,
A battledore and shuttlecock,
    A doll which can be dressed,
And one that cries out " Màmma "
    When pinched upon the chest !

A box of wooden soldiers,
　　Who *wooden't* dare to fight;
An automatic rabbit,
　　And a clockwork kind of sprite;
A Liliputian mansion,
　　With a mistress made of wax,—
Where rent is never thought of,
　　Though the house is built with *tacks* !

A moving panorama,
　　A Punch and Judy show,
A little p'rambulator,
　　That is made to *wheel or wo* !
A model grand piano,
　　On which you play a tune;
A waggon and a waggoner,
　　A miniature balloon !

A lot of cups and saucers,
　　And pots and kettles, too,
A lion and a tiger,
　　After models in the " Zoo !"
A Hansom cab and omnibus,
　　With drivers, I declare,
Who, strange to say, are satisfied
　　When they receive a fare !

A pretty little kitchen,
　　With a handsome little range;
A dolly's country residence,
　　Entitled " Holly Grange !"
And lots of my inventions
　　Have caused some first-rate fun,
And, though my list is endless,
　　My ditty now is done.　　　[*Takes seat at the table.*

Now let me see what work I've got !　　　[*Takes up letters.*
This morning's letters, what a lot !
Who's this from, with monogram so grand?　　[*Opens letter.*
An artist, Ah ! I thought I knew the hand;
He wants my aid, that's very clear.　　　　[*Reads.*
" Can you supply me with an idea,
Something within my pencil's range ! "　　[*A knock heard.*
A knock ! dear me ! that's very strange—
A visitor here is very rare;
I'm rather staggered, I declare !
I'm not too tidy, most unfortunate,
For mortals are, you know, importunate.　　[*Opens door.*

　　　Enter FLISSY *and* FLOSSY.

Two little maidens ! well, that somewhat eases me,
And I must say your visit greatly pleases me !

I thought perhaps the chimney was on fire;
Has anything so happened, may I inquire?
A sudden visit always puts me in confusion.

FLIS. *and* FLOS. Oh, Fairy, pray forgive us the intrusion!

FAIRY. Intrusion! No, indeed, my pretty creatures;
I'm very pleased to see your chubby features.
Now, what's your mission, little Miss?

FLOS. Our mission, Fairy, is just this:
We've just stepped in your Fairyship to see—

FLIS.   Two little maidens in per-plex-ity!
Suffering from ju-ven-ile *ennui*—
Two little maidens in per-plex-ity.

FLOS. We've nothing to do, we've nothing to do,
And so we've made a call on you.
Our toys are stale; we want something new.
Give us, dear Fairy, a new toy or two!

FLIS. We've lots of things at home in Eaton-square;
Of clockwork swimming dollies we've a pair;
We've a doll with lovely flaxen plaited hair,
At our nursery at home in Eaton-square.

FLOS. Our toy list's extensive,
And oh! so expensive—
At least, so dear papa and mamma do say—
Yet our nursery's dreary,
Of toys we are weary,
We're very dissatisfied, people would say.

Oh! can you help us, Fairy dear?
We're in a gloomy way;
So mamma said we'd best come here
And hear what you would say.

                              [*Repeat last four lines.*

FAIRY. In my career, it grieves me to relate,
I've found a lot of children in your state—
A state which, darlings, you've described—
And this is what I've usually prescribed;
For darlings' nursery dissatisfaction
Would almost drive the mammas to distraction;
And as their duties fairies never shirk,
I always have suggested "work!"
The crochet hook has charms, you know,
So has the needle, you'll find that sew-sew!

FLIS. *and* FLOS. For toys and play we always have contested,
And work, we grieve to say, we always have detested.

FAIRY. A sad confession! I never heard a bolder
(*Aside.*) (They will improve, no doubt, as they grow older);
But come, my darlings, I've behind this screen
Some people hidden, whom you've doubtless seen.

FLIS. *and* FLOS. Oh, Fairy! we are much obliged to you;
We only trust they may be really new.

FAIRY. Well! as to that, it must now be confessed,
They're very old, but then they're newly dressed.

There's only one or two—the number won't confuse you—
But doubtless somehow they'll amuse you.

> [FAIRY *goes to curtain and brings forth* RED RIDING
> HOOD. *Old nursery tune on the piano as she comes
> down stage.*

FLIS. *and* FLOS. Oh! Red Riding Hood, we dread her,
 Because we have so very often read her;
 But this young girl, we must confess,
 Is very nice about her dress.

FAIRY. A dress, I must say, admirably suited;
 Its novel beauty cannot be disputed,
 Designed by one I have employed again—
 An artist for the nursery—Walter Crane!
 But Riding Hood has something now to mention:
 That is if you will give her your attention.

RED RIDING HOOD'S *Story—air, first portion of "Defendant's Song"*
("Trial by Jury").

I laid for years in a dusty state,
 In a village shop near Ware,
And I lost my gloss and varnish too,
 And value, I declare!
The master thought but nought of me,
 My style, he said, was old—
In face of this indignity,
 One morning I was sold!

The lady who had purchased me
 Was kindly, I could trace,
And any little book could see
 She had a lovely face.

She sent me to her little niece,
    Who, in her usual way,
Disfigured me with dirt and grease
    In quite a shocking way!

She flung me from the window high,
    And, fluttering in the air,
A woman caught me going by,
    And treated me with care;
She took me to her sickly child,
    Who welcomed me with joy,
And many hours he beguiled
    With but a cast off toy!   [*Repeat last four lines.*

                  [RED RIDING HOOD *crosses to the left side.*

FAIRY. Some other friends, now getting active,
    May prove, perhaps, to you attractive!
            [*Goes to screen and brings* JACK HORNER *with pie.*
Jack Horner now engages your attention;
Another item, this, of my invention!
His costume is of my designing;
For plums, you see, this youth is pining!
FLIS. *and* FLOS. Jack Horner we have long ago admired;
    At present, though, he's not required.
FAIRY. Well, well! some others now we'll try,
    And leave young Horner to his pie.

    [*Goes to screen and brings forth* BO-PEEP *and rest of
        party. They enter slowly to a nursery tune, and stand
        in a half circle. The majority of the characters should
        have toys or cosaques in their hands. They sing the
        following :*

Chorus, OMNES,—*air, "Boys and Girls come out to Play."*

We've all come here to have some play—
A kind of annual holiday !
We've got a lot of things to say,
Tol-le-lol-le-lol-e-lay !

SIMPLE SIMON (*to the Tune of "Green Gravel"*).

The pieman, the pieman,
    He never is nigh,
When Simon, when Simon
    Requires a pie !

MARY (*to the air of "Jenny is a Weeping"*).

Poor Mary is contrary, contrary, contrary,
But our darling Fairy
    Will look over that.
I'll ever contrive to make my garden thrive;
You shall all have a drive,
    And see it in July.

QUEEN OF HEARTS (*sings to air, "Pop goes the Weasel!"*).

The Knave of Hearts, who stole the tarts,
    His naughty ways has seen;
And he has been forgiven by
    The pastry-cooking Queen.

KNAVE (*sings to air, "Three Blind Mice"*).

Jam tarts are nice; jam tarts are nice!
    I managed to take off two or three;
    Their flavour, oh! just suited me;
    For pastry's just the stuff for me,
Jam tarts are nice!

F

BABY BUNTING (*to air of "Baby, Baby Bunting"*).

Baby, Baby Bunting,
Dada's gone a hunting
Through the Lowther'y Arcade
For a little wooden spade!

LITTLE BO-PEEP (*to air of "Little Bo-peep"*).

Little Bo-peep, who lost her sheep,
  Has just this moment found them;
She went, you know, to the Cattle Show,
  And there it was she found them.

LITTLE MISS MUFFETT (*to air of "Little Miss Muffett"*).

Little Miss Muffett,
Who sat on a tuffet,
  Has eaten her curds and whey;
And the Fairy will guide her
From every old spider,
  And order them all away!

OMNES *repeat Chorus.*

We've all come here to have some play—
A kind of annual holiday;
And now we've said all we have to say,
Tiddy-fol-lol-de-toll-loll-lay!

FLIS. *and* FLOS. Good Fairy, we are much confused,
But cannot say that we're amused;
For though the figures which you show
Are nice, we've read them often, so
We pine for what we've never seen;
Dissatisfied we've ever been.

FLOS. Our wish has been for many days
To come across some waifs and strays—
Those haggard children, with hungry looks,
Whom we have read of in our books.
I should so like to see them, Fairy, dear!

FLIS. And so should I, if they live near!

FLOS. They live in attics, in a dingy street;
And don't have over much to eat.
Oh! Flissy; if these could be inspected,
We should not, Fairy, feel dejected.

FAIRY. I grant your wish! I am in a position
To take you there, but on condition
That afterwards no nasty traces
Of *ennui* rankle on your faces.
What is the time?

OMNES.   Nine o'clock.

FAIRY.   Oh! is it?
Then at this instant we'll make our visit.

[*Turns to row of Nursery Characters.*

And you, my friends, you have permission
To join us in our expedition.
Now on with wrapper, scarf, and muff!

[*All are busy putting on wraps, &c.*

The weather out is rather rough,
Although the Clerk is not unreasonable;
It's very cold, though, perhaps, it's seasonable.
We'll seek some dark and lonesome room,
Where poverty spreads its chill and gloom,
Where sunlight rarely finds its way,
Where children toil the livelong day,
Where food (or "wittles") would be a rarity,
Unless sent by some local charity;
Where crusts are eaten with delight,
And butter's an unusual sight;
Where coals (this p'r'aps unknown to you)
Are purchased by a pound or two;
Where children, like my Margery Daw,
Content themselves with beds of straw;

F 2

Where children (this is rare, I hope)
Are unacquainted quite with soap;
Where——but descriptions grow distressing;
Besides, my time, you know, is pressing.
Now start, my children, steadily, in pairs;
Don't run or skip, and mind the stairs!

[*The* FAIRY *stands at the door, or pulls open screen while the children pass out in pairs, the last being* FLISSY *and* FLOSSY. *As they file out, the tune of "Poor Jenny is a Weeping" should be played on the piano, slowly.*

FAIRY (*to audience*). And now to change the scene, for which I ask
Your kind indulgence for such a task.
"We beg your hearing patiently!" (Shakesperian quotation);
For detail, kindly use imagination.
I take my leave! I shall appear again
In Somewhere-court in Drury-lane.

[*Puts on cloak and fills a basket with cakes, &c., and bows herself out through the curtains to slow music.*

Curtain or folding doors.

ACT II.

SCENE—A LONESOME GARRET.

To a great extent, the scene will have to be imagined, but an old cloth can be arranged to represent dilapidated curtains, which are supposed to cover a window, and an impromptu floor could be arranged by one or two boards being laid over the carpet; the oldest furniture obtainable should be brought into use, and the stage should be darkened, the light being obtained by a candle stuck in a bottle and placed on a deal table (or, if a realistic scene is desired, French, of 89, Strand, supplies one in sheets of strong paper, which can be fitted up in a little time; they do not, however, lend them on hire). SARAH GIBLEY *and* POLLY BLAKE *should be as dirty as possible—there is not much difficulty attending that preparation—and should be in rags. As the scene opens they are discovered sitting on the floor in centre of stage, one polishing, or trying to polish, an old poker, while the other one is mending her old shoe. A portion of the air of "Pop goes the Weasel!" should be played slowly as the scene opens. A little straw and a quantity of old rags scattered about will add greatly to the effect.*

SARAH. Oh, Polly, look at this 'ere shoe!
The sole has nearly come in two;
The leather's rotten, it's weak and holely.
The question's resting on the sole now *solely.*
POLLY. Well, wot's the use of troubling about 'em?
Be like me, and do without 'em.   [*Shows her naked feet.*

If I was rich I'd allus choose
To manage without boots and shoes;
They cramps yer feet—though, I declare,
I only had my father's pair!

SARAH. Ah me! It's terribly despairing
To see your shoes beyond repairing!
Besides, these boots are such old dears,   [*Kisses her boots.*
I've had 'em such a many years!
They was my uncle's—he couldn't bear 'em,
And so he said as I could wear 'em.

POLLY. What time's mother coming home to-day?
Do you know, Sarer; did she say?

SARAH. She may be early, Poll, perhaps.

POLLY. I hope she'll bring us home some scraps!

SARAH. She's gone to Thompson's, in the square;
There'll be some scraps—they've had a party there.

POLLY. A party! Wot's that? a kind of meeting?

SARAH. Yes, only with a lot of eating,
Where there's tarts, and cakes, and all manner,
Besides a lot of playing on the pianner.

POLLY. It must be lovely! Only think—
A lot of things to eat and drink!

SARAH. They have sich lots! The Thompsons store 'em.
So mother told me—she washes for 'em.

[*POLLY gives finishing touch to poker.*

POLLY. There now, that poker, or I'm *much* mistaken,
For a new one could be taken.
A polished poker I do much admire!

SARAH. Why, wot's the use? We've got no fire!

POLLY. A fire on a day like this is very nice,
But coals are really such a price!
So mother says that we must wait
While coals are for the rich and great,
Or those like Smithson's, at the back,
Who can afford to buy a sack.

SARAH. There now, I think I'm very clever,

[*Puts on a large pair of old boots, and admires them.*

My boots now ought to last for ever!
What do you say to a game? or stay—
Let's go into the court and play!
Oh! it's raining.

POLLY.   Fast?

SARAH.   Why, yes, it pours!

[*Looks out of imaginary window.*

POLLY. Then we must find some play indoors.
Let's play at shop—now mind, play fair!
We'll have our counter on this chair.

SARAH. What kind of shop, Poll, shall it be?

POLLY. A grocer's, where they sell such lovely tea!

[*They go to the grate and get a few cinders to represent
sugar; and with buttons, bits of wood, &c., represent,
in their imagination, various articles to be found in
the grocer's emporium; they then proceed to play at
shop; meanwhile the* FAIRY *is seen to enter through
the curtain, holding the hands of* FLISSY *and* FLOSSY.
The children still proceed with the game.

FAIRY. By magic power I have entered unawares—
A wonderful accomplishment, considering the stairs!
Behold! a London garret, with occupants complete.
                                        [*To* FLISSY *and* FLOSSY.

Dost like the picture?

FLIS. *and* FLOS.   Yes! it's perfectly a treat!

FLOS. It's quite too charming! that is, we mean,
Quite different from our home, where everything is clean;
This dirt and shabbiness quite lovely looks—
It is so like the pictures in the books.
These children seem so very good;
And what nice toys! I wish we could
Play with dirt and bits of wood!

FLIS. I've often longed with cinders for to play,
But somehow nurse won't let me have my way.

FAIRY. With these poor children I'll have a conversation,
While you behind, please, take your station;
They cannot see you, for, through my ability,
I have shed over you invisibility.

FLIS. *and* FLOS. We don't know, Fairy, what you mean.

FAIRY. Well, for the present you're unseen.
Now, darlings, some attention pay,
And hear what these poor children say!

[FLISSY *and* FLOSSY *seat themselves on a stool behind,
and the* FAIRY *comes down the stage and confronts*
SARAH *and* POLLY, *who have, through the last part of
the conversation, been silently playing at shop; as
soon as the* FAIRY *stands before them they start, rise,
and make a rough curtsey.*

I've startled you—so suddenly appearing!

SARAH. We never heard you, though we're good of hearing.
Please, mother's out a charing, mum!

FAIRY. Oh! for your mother I've not come,
It is for you I've made this visit here;
I've something for you in this basket, dear.

[*Shows* SARAH *and* POLLY *basket, and proceeds to pour
out the contents into the laps of the two children, who
begin to eat voraciously.*

POLLY (*eating*). Oh! this is lovely; here's a lot!

SARAH. Oh! what a lovely tart I've got—
A currant cake, too! Look at mine!

POLLY. Ah! this is now what I calls fine.
Oh! thank you, mum, we really must,
We've only had to-day a crust!

SARAH. These thing's are nicer, I declare,
    Than wot we gets home from the square!
FAIRY. I'm glad you like them! Now pay me attention;
    Go on with your eating, I've something to mention—
    I'm a fairy!

                      [*The children look wonderingly.*

POLLY.   You're not like one of those
    I've seen in toy shops, in such lovely clothes!
    And those 'ere fairies fly on springs.
SARAH. Besides, mum, you aint got no wings.
    Are you a fairy? Well, you are a kind one!
    Afterwards we shall not mind one.
    I've never heard of fairies who have brought
    A lot of pastry up to this 'ere court.
FAIRY. Well, well, I am a fairy, though, mayhap,
    I don't possess a wand and wings to flap;
    And fairies, I would have you know,
    Don't always in bright spangles go.
    Their dresses and their actions vary,
    And I'm a very plain old fairy.
    When I was young, it must be now confessed,
    I used to walk about most grandly dressed.
    But now I'm slippery, as Shakespeare says,
    I've seen the error of my ways;
    My dresses—emblems of most youthful follies—
    I've turned now into clothes for dollies.
SARAH. Oh, Mistress Fairy, me and Poll,
    We often talk about a doll.
    We've seen 'em carried by rich little gals,
    So lovely dressed in fal-de-rals;
    And sometimes me and Polly pops
    And goes and sees 'em in the shops.
POLLY. We've never had a toy, but mother says
    She'll buy a ha'penny one, one of these days.
FAIRY. Is mother out then always, pray?
SARAH. Yes, mum, nearly every day;
    She goes a washing for folks so rich,
    They have nice houses, you never heard of sich.
    She washes for the Thompsons and the Bakers,
    And for Tympkinses, the undertakers.
FAIRY. And don't you go to school, my dear?
SARAH. The School Board man don't come up here;
    And latterly it's been so snowing,
    And Polly aint got boots to go in.
FAIRY. You think, then, you would like a doll?
SARAH. Oh yes, mum! Shouldn't we now, Poll?
    But dolls and other lovely toys
    Are only for rich girls and boys.

       [*FAIRY now goes up stage to* FLISSY *and* FLOSSY, *and
         waves her hand mystically before them, and brings
         them down to* POLLY *and* SARAH; *the ragged children*

appear awed by the sumptuous costumes of FLISSY
and FLOSSY, *who, however, kiss them, and twine their
arms round their necks.*

FAIRY. (*to audience*). I think, dear friends, you will agree
 That here a combination strange you see,
 The upper and the lower of society!
 A picture dashed with some variety.
 Here Flis. and Flos., of birth most elevated,
 Of toys are tired as they've stated;
 While they quite shock me when they say,
 With cinders they would like to play.
 They've toys of make, I'm sure, expensive
 (They mentioned this with list extensive);
 And yet, in spite of all these treasures,
 Their toys don't give them many pleasures!
 They would prefer in here to stop
 And play with dirt, or rather shop.
 The toys, on which such pains are needed,
 Are, they tell me, quite unheeded;
 That I know, because I have invented 'em,
 And just this moment I presented 'em
 With characters which, I confessed,
 Were old, but somewhat newly dressed.
 These met with little favour, as you know,
 And some were almost told to go;
 In fact, I think, I heard these children say,

     [*Pointing to* FLISSY *and* FLOSSY.

 The characters had had their day.
 These attic children, on the other hand,
 Would be delighted, as you'll understand,
 With any toy, as they have stated,
 No matter how dilapidated;
 A doll, for instance, if in sorry plight,
 Would give these children much delight.
 While Flis. and Flos., of noble station,
 In cinders would find recreation.
 To these poor children, then, shall be presented
 Some of the toys that I've invented;

     [*To* FLISSY *and* FLOSSY.

 You have some new experience to-day!
 What are you thinking of? please just say!
FLIS. I've been thinking, noble Fairy Queen,
 Of how dissatisfied we both have been.
FLOS. To think of these poor children playing all the day
 With such old toys, in such a happy way;
 While our toys are in the basket laid—
 We're very naughty, I'm afraid!
FLIS. But, oh! if something simple pa would give us,
 We should contented be (*to* FAIRY) if you'd forgive us!
FLOS. And I've a very happy notion,
 Which shall be quickly put in motion.

When I reach home, I'll ask papa's permission
To send a case of toys here, on condition
That these poor children give us, in return,
Their humble toys, for which we yearn.

                  [To SARAH and POLLY.

We've lots of dolls, some dress'd in red and blue,
And heaps of pretty things we'll send to you;
We have a tea-set and a china token,
You won't object if they're a little broken!

FAIRY. I'm glad to see this visit has improved you,
Or otherwise I ought to have reproved you.

POLLY. Oh, thank you, Miss, it's very kind of you
To think of us poor children as you do.

SARAH. And you, kind Fairy, for those cakes and such,
We thank yer ladyship very much!

      [A chorus is sung outside by the Nursery characters.

Oh, Poll, what is that? Why, I declares,
There's someone singing on the stairs!
Oh, what's just there, you'd never guess?

          [POLLY goes to the door and peeps out.

A girl in such a lovely dress!
Why, she's coming in! look at her staring!
P'r'aps she wants mother for some charing!

RED RIDING HOOD *opens the door slowly and proceeds down stage.*
The position of the figures is thus:

      RED RIDING HOOD. FAIRY.
   SARAH.   FLISSY.
   POLLY.   FLOSSY.

      [She hands to SARAH a basket, supposed
      to contain eggs, &c., and sings:

Air, "Gipsy Tent."

A basket for you, a basket for you,
With lovely eggs and buttermilk too!
Here is the basket, with ribbon so blue,
All the things in it, my dear, are for you.

      [Gives POLLY and SARAH the basket, and
      kisses them both on the forehead.

Enter SIMPLE SIMON—he has a large pie—singing to the tune of "Green
Gravel;" he sings a verse and gives the pie to POLLY.

    The pieman, the pieman,
      I caught him just by!
    So Simon, so Simon,   *[Crosses to R.*
      Has brought you a pie.

[A grotesque dance would be suitable here, if the person who represents this young man is possessed of any terpsichorean qualifications.   Nursery music should be played to bring on all these characters.

Enter JACK HORNER, *with another pie.*

My name is Jack Horner, I've come from the corner,
　You see what a very good boy am I!
For before I did come, I put in a plum,
　And now I have brought you a pie.　　　*[Crosses to* R.

Enter MARY, MARY, QUITE CONTRARY, *singing to the air of "Jenny is a-Weeping."*

Poor Mary, so contrary, contrary, contrary,
So loves her darling Fairy,
Who told her to bring,
From her garden in the square,
A bunch of flowers, oh, so rare!
For little Poll and Sarah there;
And, children, here they are!

　　　　[Presents them with flowers, and crosses to L.

Enter BABY BUNTING, *singing to the air of "Baby Bunting."*

Baby, Baby Bunting,
Dada's come from hunting;
He sent me with this pretty doll,
To give to little ragged Poll!

　　　　[Gives doll to POLL, *and crosses to* R.

Enter the QUEEN OF HEARTS, *singing to air "Pop goes the Weasel!"*

I've just come from the counting house,
　Where pa keeps all his money,
And I have brought these little girls
　A lovely pot of honey!

　　　　[Presents them with pot of honey, and crosses to L.

Enter the KNAVE OF HEARTS—*with tray of tarts—singing to the air of "Three Blind Mice."*

Oh, they're so nice! oh, they're so nice!
These beautiful tarts, on this here tray.
The Queen has bade me come and say,
They're for the little girls to-day.
Oh, aint they nice!

　　　　[Presents them with tarts, and crosses to R.

Enter LITTLE BO-PEEP, *singing to air of "Little Bo-Peep."*

You may not know me, children dear;
　By some I'm called Bo-Peep.
The Fairy's bade me come in here
　And give you this toy sheep.

　　　　[Presents them with a toy sheep and crosses to L.

Enter LITTLE MISS MUFFETT, *singing to air of " Little Miss Muffet."*

      I'm Little Miss Muffett,
      I'm Little Miss Muffett,
        You've heard of me before to-day;
      And Little Miss Muffett,
      Who sat on the tuffet,
        She gives you some curds and whey!   [*Crosses to* R.

Chorus, OMNES, *excepting* POLLY *and* SARAH—
          air, " Boys and Girls."

      We're glad to see you both to-day,
      On this our annual holiday;
      And now we think we'll have some play,
      Tiddy-fol-lol-de-lol-de-lay!

      [POLLY *then fetches from under the table an old*
        saucepan, containing their toys, such as buttons,
        clothes pegs, broken forks, bits of firewood, &c.

SARAH. Our admiration is unbounded;
      In fact, we're reg'larly astounded!
      It may be real, and yet it seems of
      Just the kind of things yer dreams of;
      To dream that you are rich, and live
      In castles, where you always give
      To poor folks sich a lot of money—
      A life, yer know, of milk and 'oney—
      And then to wake, as I've done before,
      And find yer bed a bed of straw;
      While all the castles and the money
      Is wanished!
POLLY.   Yes; it's very funny;
      But this is real, I know as much.
      The things in dreams you never can touch.
      In dreams the cakes and things are gammon,
      Not like these tarts, with lots of jam on!
      We thank ye, so, for what you've done,
      These toys will be, oh, awful fun!
SARAH. In this old saucepan here, you see
      The little things that Poll and me
      Do play with, when I'm not a scrubbing
      Floors, or Polly's not a rubbing
      Up our brasses, or preparing
      This 'ere room when mother's charing.
      They're all so shabby, and they're such——
FLIS. *and* FLOS. No matter; we should like them much!
             [*They go and inspect the saucepan of toys.*
  FLIS. Oh, the selection's lovely, I am sure!
  FLOS. Buttons! clothes pegs! who could wish for more?
      And bits of string! a match-box, too!
  FLIS. And here's a fork, and one old shoe!

FLOS. A rusty key, and some dry bones!
FLIS. And here's a lovely lot of stones!
  Oh, Fairy, we thank you much to-night!
  We think you've satisfied us quite.
  You've really done a noble action
  In finding out for us attraction.
  For in this saucepan, now before you,
  There's lots of fun, I do assure you!
  And, in return, we give them a selection
  Of our toys, if pa has no objection.
FAIRY. No; keep your toys, my children dear,
  We'll have no chopping or changing here;
  For with magic power I'm inspired,   [*To audience.*
  And I'll supply the toys required,
  To-morrow, or next day at most; [*To* SARAH *and* POLLY.
  They'll reach you by the Parcels Post—
  A good idea! There's not a better,
  The post will suit me to the letter!   [*To audience.*
  Our simple story's ended, that is clear,
  Though we are up four *storeys* here;
  We soon shall have to say "Good night!"
  And down the stairs then make our flight.
  You've been attentive, it pleases me to say,
  Whilst we've been working through our play;
  And now we've to the tag-end got,
  And plodded through the miry plot,
  It gives us players wondrous satisfaction
  To find it's been of some attraction.
  The plot is slight, but we're delighted
  To find our play has not been slighted.
  And these young friends, so full of animation,
  They thank you for your kind consideration,

  Chorus, OMNES, *"Boys and Girls, come out to Play."*
   And now we've played our little play,
   In which we've had a lot to say,
   We're quite compelled to fly away.
   We'll come again some other day!   [*Repeat.*

FAIRY. Once more, dear friends, a kind farewell!
  We're glad you've liked our play so well;
  It has amused, of that we're certain.
  There's nothing more—except the

     Curtain.

Bluebeard; or, the Cast of the Dye.

CHARACTERS.

BLUEBEARD	A Noble.
CALIPASH	The Village Barber.
FATIMA	A poor but lovely Maiden, &c.
SISTER ANNE	{ Not so pretty as her Sister, but honest, homely, and always handy.
MUSTAPHA .... POLO	} Brothers to the above, noble Youths.

COURTIERS, ATTENDANTS.

COSTUMES.

BLUEBEARD.—A turban, made of any showy material, with a robe of red or yellow twill, very wide trousers of cretonne, drawn in at ankles, and showy sash; huge scimitar, cut out of thin wood or cardboard, and covered with silver paper; beard of blue wool.

CALIPASH.—A very ragged coat, high collar, and white apron; wide trousers of coloured material, drawn in at ankles.

FATIMA.—Silk cap, short coloured bodice over skirt of cretonne, white muslin trousers, drawn in at ankles, broad sash.

SISTER ANNE.—Similar to above, only rather plainer.

MUSTAPHA AND POLO.—Large helmets, modelled in cardboard, and covered with silver paper; huge plumes, red jackets and red trousers; very large scimitars.

SCENERY.

SCENE I.—INTERIOR OF CALIPASH'S SHAVING SALOON.

Large board, with " Hair Cut in the Fashionable Style," hung up. Shelf along back of stage, with bottles, brushes, shaving pots. **If** *practicable, a scene should be painted and fastened to the frame of the window or shop door, &c.   Chairs should be placed along the stage, and, as the scene opens, CALIPASH is sitting down stropping a razor, with a very dejected air.*

SCENE II.—ANTE-ROOM ADJOINING THE BLUE CHAMBER.

Back of stage hung with curtains of cretonne or any showy material. These should be looped back slightly, and a portion of a blue door discovered (this could be painted on calico framing, primed, or on one or two sheets of cardboard).   As the fatal key figures considerably in this scene, it should be made as large as possible, say half-a-yard long. This could be easily cut out of thin wood with a fretsaw, and covered with silver paper.   Two thrones on left side.

SCENE I.—INTERIOR OF CALIPASH'S SHAVING SALOON.

CALIP. It's just struck one—the very time
When shaving should be in its prime;
All the chairs full of people, trying
My celebrated shaving, dyeing,
Singeing, sousing; or else the sportive youth,
With hanging locks, or mop uncouth,
Should be here by this time; but, alas!
Good luck from me now seems to pass
And lodge—oh! wretched fate!—
With my rival barber, Polish Pate.
Why, this sudden change of trade
Will ruin me, I am afraid!
And yet for twopence I cut hair
In just a manner, you'd declare,
To equal quite the Paris style,
Including, too, the scented "ile!"
How can I pay my taxes or my rate,
Keep house and home together, in this state
Of trade depression?   It's hardly fair;
And, as I cannot cut, I'll sing an *air.*

Song, CALIPASH—*air, " We are, we are !"*

Oh! Fortune, kindly just explain
Why you have snubbed me quite!
You've left me in the cold and rain,
And gone in for the night.

I once had customers a score,
    Not counting little boys,
But now you've sent them all next door,
    Which very much annoys!

Chorus.

    There's Mr Burke, the parish clerk;
        The baker, Mr. Brown;
    There's Mr. Black, the village quack;
        The Crier of the town;
    There's Mr. Slew, the butcher, too;
        The Overseer of Poor,
    The Pleeceman blue, and others too,
        Who've gone next door—next door!

                            [*Repeat Chorus.*

Enter FATIMA *and* SISTER ANNE.

FATIMA. Well, papa dear, and how is trade?
    Are there many fortunes being made?
  CALIP. Alas! not many, daughter fair.
    I'm afraid I want a change of *air*!
    I get so mopish. I think I'll try
    A change of air.
FATIMA (*offering him bottle*). Then why not dye—
    That's what you usually advise?
    There's nothing changes like your dyes;
    At least, this I have heard you say
    To fops, whose hair is turning grey.
  ANNE. So customers are scarce?
  CALIP.   'Tis sad to see!
    I once cut them—now they *cut* me,
    Down to the little boys, who used to wait
    Their turn from one o'clock to eight,
    Because the shop was full. 'Twas glorious fun
    To see the large amount of business done
    But now, alas!——   [*Weeps.*
FATIMA.   Oh, papa! don't go on so!
  CALIP. They patronise now this Alonso,
    Who, next door, has lately started
    A hair-dyeing es—— I shall die quite broken-hearted!
FATIMA. Come, cheer up, papa! your trade may all come back.
  CALIP. Perhaps—when I have lost my clever knack
    Of cutting, shaving, tiddivating,
    Of—there, it's very aggravating!
    I'll wait a trifle longer, and then if no
    Customers come, up the shutters go!
  ANNE. What! shut up shop?
  CALIP.   What can I do?
  ANNE. Why, take a partner or two!
    I've always understood, when businesses were dying,
    The partners came in and set them flying!
  CALIP. That's not a bad idea. But how about
    The business proofs? They call the ledger out,

Examine all the profits and the losses,
And find my business has had its crosses!
It ought not thus to be, my fortune so delaying;
But "oughts and crosses" is the game I'm always playing!

FATIMA. But, papa, don't despond! but, like a dear old dad,
Be happy!   Such sorrowing is bad.
When customers come, you'll feel much stronger.

CALIP. (*gloomily*). Yes; absence makes the hair grow longer.
That 'ere saying inspires me, my pretty Fat,
With new energy—think of that!
Who knows but that some stranger in this town
May soon, may be wandering up and down,
And want a shave, a wash up, or brush down?
I'll set my razors in a cutting trim,

[*Exit* FATIMA *and* ANNE.

And hope——

Enter BLUEBEARD.

BLUE.   Are you the barber?
CALIP. (*bowing*).   I am—a—him!
BLUE. Eh! you shave?
CALIP.   Most easily!
BLUE. Trim hair?
CALIP.   Most greasily!
BLUE. Cut corns?
            With utmost expedition!
BLUE. Improve the looks?
CALIP.   No matter what condition!
BLUE. Then trim my curls!
CALIP. (*hands chair*).   Pray, take a chair!

[*Business of sitting* BLUEBEARD *in
chair, and wrapping him in cloth.*

BLUE. (*sitting down*). I'm quite a stranger here.
CALIP. (*joyfully*).   My long-lost heir!
BLUE. (*getting up*). Your heir!   What's that you called?
I'm not your heir!
CALIP. (*bowing*).   No; see, I'm bald!
BLUE. (*sitting*). I want it cut in a fashionable style.
Have you grease?
CALIP. (*showing him bottle*). The once-deserted "ile!"
BLUE. Proceed.   Is this your usual funny way?
CALIP. I'm always *cutting*.
BLUE.   Then cut away!
I'm in a hurry—have to go away to-morrow.
CALIP. (*leaning over him while struggling to part his hair*). 'Tis the
    parting that will be such sorrow.
BLUE. (*shouting*). You're hurting me! are you aware you're stick-
    ing in
That awful comb of yours into my skin?

[CALIPASH *finishes* BLUEBEARD, *who rises from chair,
and starts on seeing* FATIMA, *who enters at this point.*

BLUE. (*pointing to Fat.*).   Is this your charge?
CALIP.   Sixpence is my *fee*, Sir.
BLUE. (*aside to Calip.*).   Tut, tut! I mean this girl.
CALIP.   Oh! she's—er——
BLUE. Your daughter, your niece, mother or cousin?
CALIP. My daughter—one of a dozen.
BLUE. And she's the youngest, I suppose?
CALIP. Well, let me see, there's Angelina, Rose,

> [*Counting on his fingers.*

Floriline, Vaseline, Clementina, Concertina,
Sophorina—have you seen her?—
Sewingmachina, &c., &c.   That's Fatima—
She's the youngest; I thought she was!
BLUE. You thought!
CALIP.   I thought " becus "
She eats the most.
BLUE.   Speak not thus of her, I pray.
Introduce me!
CALIP. (*holding his hand out*).   Yes, Sir—when you pay.
BLUE. (*gives him a coin*).   Well, there's your fee!
CALIP.   A guinea! Oh! most soothing balm,
You very rarely cross my palm!
(*To* BLUEBEARD.) But let me thank you kindly for this
  gift.
BLUE. Introduce me to her!
CALIP. (*aside*).   That's his drift!
He's rich—perhaps some lord or earl.
Who knows but that my girl
Might win him, wed him, woo him?
Good! I'll introduce her to him.
(*Taking them both by the hand.*) Allow me, Fatima, my dear,
  to introduce you to
This gentlemen, my daughter true,
Whose name is er—Mr. Smith—no doubt you've 'eard.
BLUE. (*disgusted, aside to* CALIPASH). Mr. Smith! Bah! my name's
  Bluebeard.
CALIP. Fatima—Bluebeard.   (*To* FATIMA.) Smile, you ninny!
(*Aside to* FATIMA.) It isn't every man who pays a guinea
To have his hair curled, trimmed, or cut.
FATIMA. But he's so hideous!
CALIP.   Hideous! tut, tut!
Looks are nothing, silly pate,
So start a weather tête-à-tête!
Bring out all your learning, science, art;
Do everything to win his heart!
FATIMA. Win his heart?
CALIP.   That's what I propose.
FATIMA. With what result?
CALIP.   Buy us new clothes—
Move to a better shop—leave this hole—
Buy a parrot and a barber's pole;

While you will be a lady!

FATIMA.   That's very true;
But don't you see his beard is blue?

CALIP. That's in his favour. You'd make a handsome pair.
He's no doubt a prince in his country over there.

Concerted Piece, BLUEBEARD, FATIMA, CALIPASH—*air, "Consum-*
mately utter!" (C. Sheard, Holborn).

BLUE. Oh! pretty Fatima, I pray,
        You'll kindly take to me!
    Such beauty, lady, let me say,
        Is quite too lover-lee.

FATIMA. I'm sure you're versed quite in the art
        Of flattering our sex!

CALIP. (*aside to* FATIMA.) Don't talk like that, you'll break my heart;
        It's very wrong to vex.

BLUE. I'm anxious to marry a beauty like you.

FATIMA. But pray just explain why your beard is so blue!

CALIP. Don't treat him so coldly, but answer him boldly,
        Or else, Miss, your conduct will come home to you!

                    [*Repeat Chorus, and finish with following,*
                            sung to melody of Chorus.

BLUE. I'll lay at your feet all the fortune I've got!

CALIP. I'll have a new brush and a new shaving pot!

FATIMA. I know you so slightly. (*To* CALIP.) He's very unsightly!

CALIP *to* FATIMA. I say he's handsome.

FATIMA.   I say he's not!

                    [*Repeat.* FATIMA *walks up stage.*

BLUE. How does my suit proceed? Oh, Sir! alack!
    Does she favour?

CALIP.   This is but the first attack.
    Why not woo yourself? It's always been admitted——

BLUE. That I should press my suit?

CALIP.   Well, you're best *fitted.*

BLUE. She cannot cast me off—she can't say "no!"
    To such a handsome man, so *comme il faut* ;
    So versed in all the arts that go
    To win the *hearts* of high and low.

                    [*With a satisfied look, and musing*
                            as he looks in a pocket mirror.

    Pink of perfection! Well, it's true.

CALIP. (*aside*). *Pink?* let's rather say he's blue!

BLUE. Come hither, ancient barber man,
And list while I unfold my plan !
You see my beard—a most decided hue—
Has often proved a great obstruction to
My progress in all matters of the heart.
Are you listening ?

CALIP.   I 'art.

BLUE. Useless all efforts to remove the tint !
I've tried bi-chloride, tri-chloride, and peppermint ;
Almond rock, postman's knock, oil, and buttered toast ;
Clothes-line, and chlorodyne, soap, and parcels post ;
Oil of castor, sticking plaster, Hudson's Patent Soap—
And all without success ! So now I've given up all hope !

CALIP. A very painful case !

BLUE.   It is for me, Sir.

CALIP. Pray, have you ever tried the tweezer ?

BLUE. I've tried everything, as I'm a man !
Nothing will remove it !

CALIP.   Try a light spring van !

BLUE. (catches CALIPASH by throat). My temper, Sir, you'll soon be
        proving ;
Vans, indeed !

CALIP.   Well, they do moving.

BLUE. But, coming to the plan. What if I load your daughter
With presents that should win her ?

CALIP.   It ought ter !

BLUE. Then I'll send round this evening, by my valet,
The richest things !

CALIP. (joyfully).   Of untold "vally!"

BLUE. Laces, silks, jewels, furs—in fact,
I'll send a box quite fully packed.
Then, if she's smitten by the presents rare,
Coax her for the marriage to prepare ;
I'll give a thousand guineas for her trousseau !
Is that a bargain (shaking hands) ?

CALIP.   It is so !

Chorus, BLUEBEARD and CALIPASH—air, " Oh ! what a wicked young
Man you are !"

BLUE. (to FAT.). Oh ! do, do say the word !
FAT. Well, you had better consult papa !
CAL. Yes, yes ! do say the word !
Oh ! what a tiresome girl you are !
[Repeat Chorus, and Curtain.

SCENE II.—ANTE-ROOM ADJOINING BLUE CHAMBER.

BLUEBEARD *and* FATIMA *discovered sitting on throne,* COURTIERS *kneeling before them.*

Chorus of COURTIERS—*air, "Stay with me, Johnnie"*
(Francis Bros. and Day).

Pray, do not linger!
Your train is due,
At Barbe Bleu Station,
To bear you to
The land where stern duty
Calls you away;
Pray, do not linger!
No longer stay!

[*They rise and stand in two lines, thus* ╱ ╲
down stage, showing Blue Chamber.

Enter CALIPASH, *an awful swell, Imperial Grand Barber to* BLUE-
BEARD, *apron on, with large comb and brush in his hand.*

BLUE. Ah! good Calipash, the parting's near at hand.
CALIP. (*looking at his comb*). The *parting!* I don't understand.
BLUE. You've forgotten my journey, I'm afraid.
CALIP. Your journey! I was thinking of my trade.
I wish you well! Till you come back
For pleasure we shall be quite slack;
No one to lead the dinner or the dance
While you are journeying to South of France,
Timbuctoo, Highgate too, Hampstead Heath;
Up in a balloon, and through tunnels underneath;
In and out, round about, over hill and dale,
Up to Vesuvius by the Vesuvian Mail;
Over cliff, mountain stiff—mode of climbing funny,
Down in dell, down again, down to even money!

[BLUEBEARD *and* FATIMA *come down stage.*

BLUE. That won't take me long. So now, farewell,
Sweet Fatima! 'twill be a spell
Of misery to both of us, this absence, though
'Twill be but short, most surely so!

But, 'ere I start, I give you these—
My ring of little household keys.
This for my larder; this, you will see,
Is for the garret—there's the "G";
This for the stables, the coach-house, and the attic;
This one for the shower-bath.

CALIP.   That sounds rheumatic!

BLUE. This for the harness cupboard—give it to the groom;
This for my uncle's, and my ante-room;
These are for the parlour, the yellow and the red rooms,
The roasting-jack, the third floor back, and bed rooms;
This for my watch—mind, keep it on the tick;
And this is someone's key to arithmetic;
Your father's room—here, take your key, Sir!—
And this one's for my hot-water geyser—
The key to wealth and fortune dear;

                          [*Brings out large key,*
And this for—the Blue Chamber here!

                  [*A little slow music on piano at this point.*
But, mark you well, and bear attention to
What I forbid you in my absence do!
Go not into that chamber! even more,
I charge thee, go not near the door!
Once get the key inserted in the lock, and sure!
My Fatima will be no more;
For death is the penalty, without delay,

                          [*Gives* FATIMA *the key.*
No matter what the time or day!
So bear in mind my dread command.
And now to start! How do we stand
For time?

CALIP.   A second longer, and you'll lose the train!

BLUE. Good! Well then, farewell all, once again!
I leave by the west gate; so, Fatima fair,
Attend and bid good-bye from there!

         [*A slow march is played, and then all file out,* COURTIERS
            first, CALIPASH *with* SISTER ANNE, *and* BLUEBEARD
            and FATIMA *in the rear. Directly the procession is
            clear of stage, re-enter* CALIPASH.

CALIP. He's gone at last—the parting o'er!
Bluebeard, my recent son-in-law.
He's very nice, but somehow, still,
I always feel a kind of chill
When he is in the way. There comes o'er me stealing
A kind of something, awful feeling!
He's so ferocious, got such an awful eye,
A kind of one you can't pass by!
It is his and not all my eye! (*Tragically.*)
What is this rumour I've lately heard,
About a room with bodies?—bah—absurd!

[Looks about timidly.

And yet, why should this room here
Be kept so sealed from Fatima dear ?
It's getting dark (*looks round*). I wish my nerves were
 stronger;
It's no go, I can't stay in here longer!

[Exit hurriedly in a terrified state.

Enter FATIMA, *key in hand.*

FATIMA. The fatal chamber and the fatal key,
On which hangs—yes—the life of me !
'Tis hard to be in such a plight,
Halting 'twixt wrong and right.
If I do right, I pass the chamber o'er;
If I do wrong, I open wide the door !
And though not right to be a *wrong doer,*
It's only human, they say, to err.
Does Bluebeard think it kindness to her,
His wife, when he goes on his tour,
By leaving such a charge ! (*cries*) booh-er—booh-er!
What is inside ? I oft have pondered,
Thought about it, mystified myself, and wondered ;
Tried to peep through keyhole, creak or crack,
But never could a glimpse obtain, alack !
I've stolen glances from the garden, but I find
The windows thickly curtained—no doubt, as a *blind.*
What can it hold, this awful room ?
It seems to fill me quite with gloom,
To live in a mansion, and know not what
People in the front room we have got.
Oh, pretty key ! would I were you,
That little keyhole to look through!
Now, tell me what in that chamber blue
There is to see; now tell me, do !
No answer ! In fairy tales this key would speak
When information one would seek ;
(*To key.*) But this key's cold, as one can feel ;
Oh, Sir, you have a heart of steel !

  *[She looks round to see if anyone is near; then, on tiptoe,
  glides slowly towards the blue doors; she peeps through
  the keyhole.*

Like most keyholes, the other side is blocked,
Or else with dirt and dust got overstocked.

  *[She hesitates, and comes down stage half frightened, and
  looks about, then again to the keyhole.*

I might just open it for a second, say,
Then shut it quickly, and run away !
There's no one near; suppose I do!   *[Looks round.*
So, here goes—one—two—   *[Putting key in lock.*

The lock's rusty—it grinds and creaks, too;
This is one of the creaks I couldn't see through.
At last, the lock has given.   And so—

> [*Takes out key, and as she opens the door the lights are
> darkened and a series of moans heard; she drops the
> key and rushes from the stage.*

Oh, horror! Mercy! Let me go! Let me go!   [*Exit.*

Enter CALIPASH *with a lantern and a nightcap on, walks slowly.*

CAL. I've bolted up (the work is tiring)
All the doors before retiring;
For there are some burglarious men
Who'd beard this lion in his den.
This chamber's at it again, trying to infuse   [*Shivering.*
The awful malady known as the Blues;
I would not sleep in here, no not
For all the gold Bluebeard has got!   [*Yawns.*
Ugh! I'll get up to bed, and try
To rest my weary, weary eye.

> [*Goes up to door, and is startled to find
> it open.*

Hullo! the door's ajar; 'twas locked this minute;
But as it's ajar I'll see what's in it!

> [*Steps in, and rushes out with all his
> hair streaming, and falls down on centre
> of stage.*

Hi! help! Servants, Courtiers, Guards!

> [*Moans as before.*

Here's the Chamber of Horrors from Madame Tussaud's!
Help! hi! ho! ho!

> [*Curtain drawn for a minute, while he is kicking on the
> stage, to enable him to get off. The curtain is drawn
> back, and enter* CALIPASH *and* FATIMA *with key,
> rubbing with emery cloth.*

CALIP. It's no use rubbing! I've rubbed with all my might,
And still the stain remains in sight.
I've scrubbed it, rubbed it, burnt it, filed it,
Since with the gore, Miss, you defiled it,
By dropping near the chamber door
This fatal key upon the floor.
Through this mishap we shall be poorer—
To you and me an awful floorer!
FATIMA (*crying*) Oh, woe is me! The fatal door!
CALIP. Why didn't you "whoa" before?
No use! the stain of blood still remains;

> [*Sinks down exhausted.*

This is the stainiest of stains

Duet, FATIMA *and* CALIPASH—*air, " Over the Garden Wall."*

CHORUS.

CALIP. Fatima, Fatima, we're in a plight,
     All through this awful key;
     I've been rubbing it all day and night!
     Oh, what an awful key!
FATIMA. I've tried Cockle's Pills, and Syrup of Squills,
     Oh, what an awful key!
     But the stain is there still, I feel dreadful chills,
     All through this awful key!

Chorus, BOTH.

     Oh, what an awful key!
     There is the stain, just see!
     We've rubbed it night, and rubbed it day,
     And still the stain won't go away.
     Oh, what a penny we both shall pay,
     All through this awful key!

FATIMA. Horror! Bluebeard returned!   Ah! that's his cough!
  CALIP. (*timidly.*) Come back already? Then I'm off!

                                        [*Exit* CALIPASH.

Enter BLUEBEARD, *with rugs and portmanteau.*

  BLUE. Well, how have you behaved?   Come, take my bag!
     Come, hurry, Fatima! you dawdle and you lag!
FATIMA. Behave, Sir! you treat me like a child!
     I cannot bear such treat——

BLUE. (*In a surly, furious mood*).   Bear! I'm wild!
    Bad luck has followed my journey through,
    Dogging my footsteps, as stray dogs do,
    O'er land and sea, mountain, valley and park,
    It dogged my footsteps, even on the barque!
    No riches could I muster! Instead, I lost,
    As you, Fatima, will learn to your cost.
    So down go household, and your own expenses!
    To-day our short-ration season commences.
    No parties, dances, dinners, teas!
    Leave me; and also leave the keys!

    [*A pause, during which* BLUEBEARD *is losing his temper.*

FATIMA (*frightened, handing bunch of keys*). Please, Sir, here you
    are; you'll find them right!
BLUE. (*counting them*). Hem! yes. Why are you so white?
    (*Catching hold of her wrist.*) You tremble like a leaf! What
    have you done
    In my leave of absence, timid one?   [FATIMA *here sobs.*
    This bunch is perfect. But let me see
    My much admired little key
    For yonder door! Come, no delay! [*Snatches key from her.*
    What's this you're hiding in your hand, Miss, pray?
    Ha! ha! ho! ho! Stained! So, so!
    You thought you'd in the chamber go!
FATIMA (*on her knees*). Mercy! spare me! Mercy! Oh!
BLUE. Prepare for death in a second or so!
    Mercy? I know not the meaning of the word!
    After what you've done, why it's absurd
    To ask! So tremble! Bid farewell to your pa,
    While I go and sharpen up my scimitar!

                            [*Exit* BLUEBEARD, *tragically*, R.

Enter CALIPASH *and* SISTER ANNE.

FATIMA. Oh, fatal key! I'm lost! I'm lost!
    Oh, curiosity! at what a cost
    Have I thee purchased! Oh, wretched drop!
CALIP. In future purchase at another shop!
    Oh! why did you do it, my gentle daughter?
BLUE. (*without*). You've got a second and a quarter!
FATIMA. Go, sister Anne, up to the northern turret,
    And search for help, or scream "fur it!"   [*Exit* ANNE, L.
CALIP. Oh! wretched key! why did you drop it?
BLUE. (*without*). My sword will do. Now I'll just strop it!
FATIMA. Oh! sister Anne, what do you see, please say!
SIS. ANNE (*without*). Two horsemen riding fast this way;
    I've waved my 'kerchief—the signal they have seen!
    They've reached the mountains, and now the green!
    The castle ruins now they've got through!

Enter BLUEBEARD, *sharpening his sword on a razor strop.*

BLUE. Now then, Fatima, receive your due!

Go, Calipash, no longer tarry,
But use it as a lesson when your other girls marry!

CALIP. If I was younger I'd have a tussle;
But I'm shelled out—got no muscle.   [*Exit weeping.*

BLUE. Now for it!

[*He catches hold of her wrists, and she struggles and
screams on her knees; he lifts up the sword, and is
slowly bringing it down, when POLO and MUSTAPHA
enter; they have a terrific struggle with BLUEBEARD,
and finally stab him.*

BLUE. (*on the ground*). I die! I die!

Enter CALIPASH, SISTER ANNE, and COUNTESS.

CAL.   His last confession!
It was always somehow my impression
That his beard was not of natural hue,
And, as he says, he dyes! It's true
You have succeeded, Sons!   [*Points to BLUEBEARD.*

MUST. *and* POLO.   We never fail!

CAL. (*timidly*). Is he dead?

MUST.   As a Blue Chamber door nail!

FATIMA. Saved! Oh! thanks, my Brothers, dear!

CALIP. You might as well, now you are here,
Stop to supper—stop here for the night,
Since now our future looks so bright!

Finale, OMNES—air, "We won't go Home till Morning"
(Howard and Co., Marlborough Street).

CHORUS. *Tempo di valse.*

Our story is ended, we're happy to say,
    In a manner that's pleasing to all.
So now we'll enjoy ourselves in such a way,
    And drive away envy and gall!
We'll have a good supper, and keep it up late,
    There's nothing at all to be feared,
We'll have apple pie, and ever will try
    To forget about nasty Bluebeard!

Chorus.

We won't break up till morning,
Till early day is dawning,
Until we all are yawning!
    And then we'll go to bed.

Curtain.

www.ingramcontent.com/pod-product-compliance
Lightning Source LLC
Chambersburg PA
CBHW081518040426
42447CB00013B/3258